William Carlos Williams

AND ROMANTIC IDEALISM

Recipient of the Brown University Press
First Book Prize Award.

Wood engraving by Barry Moser

William Carlos Williams

AND ROMANTIC IDEALISM

Carl Rapp

 Published for Brown University Press by
University Press of New England
HANOVER AND LONDON, 1984

UNIVERSITY PRESS OF NEW ENGLAND

BRANDEIS UNIVERSITY	UNIVERSITY OF NEW HAMPSHIRE
BROWN UNIVERSITY	UNIVERSITY OF RHODE ISLAND
CLARK UNIVERSITY	TUFTS UNIVERSITY
DARTMOUTH COLLEGE	UNIVERSITY OF VERMONT

LIBRARY OF CONGRESS CATALOGING IN PUBLICATION DATA

Rapp, Carl, 1946–
William Carlos Williams and romantic idealism.

Includes bibliographical references and index.
1. Williams, William Carlos, 1883–1963—Criticism and
interpretation. 2. Romanticism. 3. Idealism in literature. I. Title.
PS3545.I544Z872 1984 811'.52 83-40561
ISBN 0-87451-290-5

Where is the Existence Out of Mind or Thought Where is
it but in the Mind of a Fool.

—BLAKE, *A Vision of The Last Judgment*

To my mother and father

Contents

A Note on Texts

In the following pages, quotations from the writings of Emerson are taken from *The Centenary Edition of the Complete Works of Ralph Waldo Emerson*, ed. Edward Waldo Emerson, 12 vols. (Boston: Houghton, Mifflin, 1903–04), and are identified by parenthetical references to the abbreviation *CE* followed by the appropriate volume and page numbers. However, whenever possible I have cited instead, using the abbreviation *CW*, *The Collected Works of Ralph Waldo Emerson*, I, eds. Robert E. Spiller and Alfred R. Ferguson (Cambridge: Harvard Univ. Press, 1971) and *The Collected Works of Ralph Waldo Emerson*, II, eds. Joseph Slater, Alfred R. Ferguson, and Jean Ferguson Carr (Cambridge: Harvard Univ. Press, 1979).

Texts of Williams' work are cited by using the following abbreviations:

ARI   *A Recognizable Image: William Carlos Williams on Art and Artists*, ed. Bram Dijkstra (New York: New Directions, 1978)

A   *The Autobiography of William Carlos Williams* (New York: New Directions, 1967)

CEP   *The Collected Earlier Poems of William Carlos Williams* (New York: New Directions, 1951)

EK   *The Embodiment of Knowledge*, ed. Ron Loewinsohn (New York: New Directions, 1974)

I   *Imaginations: Kora in Hell, Spring and All, The Great American Novel, The Descent of Winter, A Novelette and Other Prose*, ed. Webster Schott (New York: New Directions, 1970)

IAG   *In the American Grain* (New York: New Directions, 1956)

IWCW   *Interviews with William Carlos Williams*, ed. Linda

Welshimer Wagner (New York: New Directions, 1976)

P   *Paterson* (New York: New Directions, 1963)

PB   *Pictures from Brueghel and Other Poems* (includes *The Desert Music and Other Poems* and *Journey to Love*) (New York: New Directions, 1962)

SE   *Selected Essays of William Carlos Williams* (New York: New Directions, 1969)

SL   *The Selected Letters of William Carlos Williams*, ed. John C. Thirlwall (New York: McDowell, Obolensky, 1957)

Divisions between lines of poetry quoted from *Pictures from Brueghel* are indicated by a double solidus separating one triadic line from another and a solidus separating each of the three components within the triad.

Acknowledgments

This book could not have been written without the stimulation and encouragement I have received from teachers, friends, and colleagues. To J. Hillis Miller I owe the largest debt of thanks, since it was his teaching and his writing that inspired me to embark on this project in the first place, just as it was his continued interest and advice that enabled me to see it through to the end. In the early stages of writing, I profited considerably from suggestions and comments made by John Edward Hardy, Ralph J. Mills, Jr., Julian Breslow, William V. Davis, and Stan Scott—all former colleagues of mine at the University of Illinois at Chicago Circle. More recently, my colleagues at the University of Georgia, including especially Marion Montgomery, James B. Colvert, E. C. Bufkin, Walter Gordon, Charles Patterson, Edward Krickel, Warren Leamon, Coburn Freer, and Betty Jean Craige, have helped me enormously by reading and criticizing various portions of the manuscript. David A. Edwards, of the Department of Mathematics, has also contributed to this book, not only by reading the manuscript but also by sharing with me, in many conversations, his keen interest in a wide range of intellectual matters, including the philosophical issues which are necessarily touched on in my efforts to explain Williams' poetry. Finally, my wife, Susan, has helped me immeasurably by continuing to believe in the worth of this project and, most important, by continuing to believe in my ability to bring it to a successful conclusion.

1 Idealism and the Vision of "The Wanderer"

I form ideas, I have perceptions, and here there is a certain definite content, as, for instance, this house, and so on. They are my perceptions, they present themselves to me; I could not, however, present them to myself if I did not grasp this particular content in myself, and if I had not posited it in a simple, ideal manner in myself. Ideality means that this definite external existence, these conditions of space, of time, and matter, this separateness of parts, is done away with in something higher; in that I know this external existence, these forms of it are not ideas which are mutually exclusive, but are comprehended, grasped together in me in a simple manner.

 —HEGEL, *Lectures on the Philosophy of Religion*

I always knew that I was I, precisely where I stood and that nothing could make me accept anything that had no counterpart in myself by which to recognize it.

 —WILLIAMS, "The Basis of Faith in Art"

In recent years, it has been customary in discussions of William Carlos Williams to stress the special importance of his early poem "The Wanderer." First published in *The Egoist* in 1914 and ultimately accorded the status of proem in *The Collected Earlier Poems*, "The Wanderer" reflects the influence not only of Keats but also of Whitman. In itself, this is enough to make the poem seem especially noteworthy, since, prior to "The Wanderer," Williams appears to have kept his Whitman-like notebooks separate from his imitations of Keats, being convinced apparently that his two favorite poets were essentially incompatible. However, most critics go so far as to claim that the effect of the poem is to show that by 1914 Whitman had displaced Keats as a major influence on Williams. For these critics, "The Wanderer" marks a crucial turning point in Williams' development, the point at which he stopped trying to be "romantic" and accepted his true vocation as a poet of reality, a poet of raw, unmediated experience, more or less after the fashion of Whitman.

Thus, according to Richard Macksey, "The Wanderer" is "the first genuine rite of passage" in Williams' poetry, since it carries him beyond the rather Keatsian alienation "implied by the title and records a total immersion" in "the immediate world." Henceforth, says Macksey, Williams becomes a poet of "unmediated and instantaneous sensation," for whom "any transcendence beyond the immediate field of experience is unthinkable."[1] For similar reasons, James Breslin finds "The Wanderer" "crucial to any study of [Williams'] development." In this "self-consciously anti-romantic" poem, Breslin argues, Williams "renounces the dreamy ideality of the aesthete and identifies himself with the 'filthy' but generative reality of the here and now."[2] Joseph N. Riddel, in his essay "The Wanderer and the Dance: William Carlos Williams' Early Poetics," describes the poem's protagonist (who clearly stands for Williams himself) as a character who ultimately seeks "to harmonize himself with the given," a character "ruled by contingency, by immediacy, and thus by the present ground where he wanders."[3] Riddel makes the point again in his book *The Inverted Bell*, where he defines Williams' wanderer as "one deprived of all hope of self-transcendence, or even of an identity apart from place, of a self apart from the field it walks, and takes intimate measure of, or designs."[4]

It must be said, however, that the most compelling version of this particular interpretation of the poem and its consequences for Williams' later work is to be found in J. Hillis Miller's essay on Williams in *Poets of Reality*. According to Miller, "The Wanderer" celebrates a "homecoming" that makes the rest of Williams' poetry "possible."[5] In describing his symbolic plunge into the rotten depths of the Passaic River, Williams renounces forever the "private consciousness" or "ego" so dear to the romantic poet. "To give up the ego," explains Miller, "means to give up also those dramas of subject and object, self and world, which have long been central in Western literature and philosophy." Since in Miller's view romantic poetry is largely based on "an opposition between the inner world of the subject and the outer world of things," and since "The Wanderer," in essence, describes the final, ecstatic merger of subject and object, it follows that the poem must take Williams "beyond romanticism." Indeed, it takes him even further, for it also takes him beyond the major Western traditions of dualism (the Christian and Platonic traditions, for example) with all their distinctions between "this" world and the "other" world, between heaven and earth, God and man, being and becoming, reality and appearance. As a result, themes of estrangement or alienation virtually disappear from Williams' poetry as do the typically romantic motifs of aspiration or desire. All of these things vanish because Williams refuses to entertain any longer the notion of a reality that is distant or "other." As the instrument in verse of this profoundly radical gesture, "The Wanderer" represents (to use Miller's terms) "a revolution in human sensibility."

To say that Miller's view of Williams has been particularly influential would be an understatement, for it has been truly seminal. Almost everyone who has had anything to say about the subject since 1965 has been forced to come to terms with Miller's view in one way or another, and it remains, on the whole, the most stimulating conception of Williams yet to appear. The reason is that

Miller makes Williams out to be a figure of decisive importance in the history of modern poetry. As Miller reads him, Williams somehow managed to outstrip his contemporaries in the sense that he was able to circumvent some of the problems that continued to give them trouble. Yeats, Eliot, and Stevens become in Miller's interpretation poets in transition who spend the better part of their careers trying to extricate themselves from the dilemmas of romanticism. Only at the very end do they arrive at positions comparable to the one Williams seems to have reached as early as 1914. Consequently, it is Williams alone, among the poets of his generation, who has the time to explore the world of immanence or presence that opens up after romanticism has been overcome.

Indeed, Miller's insight into the differences between Williams and the other modern poets has evidently inspired some of the recent attempts to define what is now called "postmodernism," with the result that Williams has emerged more clearly than ever as a sort of patron saint of the reaction against "modernist" aesthetics that occurred in the 1950s and the 1960s.[6] The distinction Miller draws in *Poets of Reality* between romanticism and modernism is now being drawn, in some circles, between modernism itself and postmodernism. The so-called "high" modernists have been reinterpreted in such a way that they now seem less like enemies of romanticism and more like unwitting participants in the romantic tradition, so that, if a revolution in sensibility such as Miller describes can be said to have occurred at all, it is perhaps more plausible to say that it occurred in the transition from modernism to postmodernism. In any case, it is clear that the term "postmodern" has been used of late to denote a position that Williams is supposed to have occupied from about 1914 on.[7]

What are we to make of the rather extraordinary claim that Williams and his fellow modernists (or, as some would say, Williams and the postmodernists) have engaged in "a revolution in human sensibility"? There is no question that this claim has been responsible for stimulating a whole new wave of interest in Williams, and for that one can only be grateful. But it has also distracted attention away from the fact that Williams does indeed have strong ties with the traditions he is supposed to have transcended. For example, as I shall try to show in the pages that follow, Williams' conceptions of poetry and experience are very similar to those of Emerson. In fact, I should say that Williams more nearly resembles Emerson's idea of a poet than any other poet we have had since Emerson, including Whitman, Stevens, and Crane. This does not mean Williams is not revolutionary. To resemble Emerson is, by definition, to be revolutionary. But it does mean that Williams cannot be properly understood apart from two major nineteenth-century traditions: romanticism and idealism. We should not, therefore, be surprised to find numerous affinities between his work and the work of other writers in these traditions. And this means, in turn, that Williams is inevitably involved in the parent of these traditions, which Miller refers to as the Christian or Platonic tradition. Although one hears almost daily of a philosopher or a poet or even a theologian who has gone beyond this tradition, I cannot see that such is the case with Williams. In his book *Natural Supernaturalism*, M. H. Abrams has shown how the essential lineaments of this Western tradition persist covertly in the work of some of the most radical, and radically secular, writers and thinkers of the last two hundred years—and Williams, I would argue, participates in this tradition in much the same way they do. Obviously, no sane reader would call him a Christian or a Platonist in the usual sense, but, because he is so deeply attached to his own version of the myth of the fall, Williams cannot help but express a variety of opinions and prejudices that are reminiscent both of Christian theology and Platonism. What is now needed, therefore, is an acknowledgment of the ways in which Williams recapitulates certain aspects of the work of his predecessors.

Since "The Wanderer" is the poem which is supposed to express Williams' departure from all these traditions, it serves as an appropriate starting point. One important question that needs to be answered is this: How can a poem so obviously dependent on Keats be said to precipitate its author beyond romanticism? The prevailing view of "The Wanderer" makes sense, I think, only if the exuberant Whitman-like affirmation of "this" world, with which the poem concludes, is really anti-Keatsian or antiromantic. In fact, it is not. However much "The Wanderer" reminds one of Whitman's poems ("Crossing Brooklyn Ferry," for example, or "This Compost"), the true inspiration behind it seems to have been Keats's Hyperion fragments. And, if we look closely at these poems, we find that Williams' poem does not imply anything essentially different from what they imply about the nature of the poet and the objects of the poet's experience. Whether he knew it or not, in writing "The Wanderer," Williams was affirming an essentially romantic conception of his own vocation.

"The Wanderer" is the story of the development of Williams' awareness of himself as a poet. In his relationship to the ugly goddess who acts as his mentor in the poem, the narrator recapitulates the relationship between Apollo and Mnemosyne in "Hyperion" and also, of course, the relationship between the narrator and Moneta in "The Fall of Hyperion." As Williams' poem begins, the narrator finds himself facing the same problem his Keatsian counterparts face: he is not altogether sure who he is or what his place is to be in the world around him. Crossing the ferry into New York, he sees before him "the great towers of Manhattan," and he asks himself rather diffidently, "How shall I be a mirror to this modernity?" (*CEP*, 3). This question suggests at the very outset that the fledgling poet who asks it has not yet found a satisfactory way to relate himself to the external world, particularly the world of the city. That he desires at least some sort of relation is evident from the fact that he is already moving in the direction of "the great towers." Quite suddenly, however, he is distracted from his thoughts by the appearance of a strange goddess who calls to him from the water, and then, unaccountably, disappears into the sky in the form of "a great sea-gull." Dazzled and excited, the young poet-to-be turns away from the city, his original destination, to pursue the goddess:

> "Come!" cried my mind and by her might
> That was upon us we flew above the river
> Seeking her, grey gulls among the white—
> (*CEP*, 4)

From this point on in the poem, the goddess alone—not the city—becomes the object of his concentrated attention:

"I am given," cried I, "now I know it!
I know now all my time is forespent!
For me one face is all the world!
For I have seen her at last, this day,
In whom age in age is united—
Indifferent, out of sequence, marvelously!
Saving alone that one sequence
Which is the beauty of all the world, for surely
Either there in the rolling smoke spheres below us
Or here with us in the air intercircling,
Certainly somewhere here about us
I know she is revealing these things!"
And as gulls we flew and with soft cries
We seemed to speak, flying, "It is she
The mighty, recreating the whole world,
This is the first day of wonders!

(*CEP*, 4)

Williams (or the narrator) apparently takes the goddess to be a kind of logos that manifests itself in all things as a single principle. The ambiguity of her status, however, makes him conceive of her as an alternative to the "modernity" that previously concerned him, and so he declares: "I will take my peace in her henceforth!" When she turns his attention back to the city in the third section of the poem, he finds it repellent:

There came crowds walking—men as visions
With expressionless, animate faces;
Empty men with shell-thin bodies
Jostling close above the gutter,
Hasting—nowhere!

(*CEP*, 5)

Just at this moment, he sees her for the first time as she really is— "ominous, old, painted"—a ghastly figure of a woman, yet strangely alluring. At the same time, he tells us "she had covered / The godhead" to go beside him. This statement makes it difficult to determine whether she is beautiful or ugly. Is she to be identified with "the beauty of all the world" or with the repulsive city dwellers, or both? Could it be that the "shell-thin" men are empty because they are ignorant of the goddess? As soon as this last thought occurs to him, the narrator offers to become her prophet. "Marvelous old queen," he shouts,

> Grant me power to catch something of this day's
> Air and sun into your service!
> That these toilers after peace and after pleasure
> May turn to you, worshippers at all hours!"
>
> (CEP, 5)

It is clear, however, that the narrator's real interest is in the goddess herself, not in the toilers. "To you," he pleads, "give me always a new marriage":

> May I be lifted still, up and out of terror,
> Up from before the death living around me—
> Torn up continually and carried
> Whatever way the head of your whim is,
> A burr upon those streaming tatters—
>
> (CEP, 6)

Her response to his appeals, however, is either derision or enigmatic silence.

In the fourth section of the poem, called "The Strike," she again forces him to contemplate the city (this time Paterson, where disgusting proletarians are standing dismally in breadlines). This time, his reaction is peculiarly intense. The crowd to him is "Ugly, venomous, gigantic":

> The flat skulls with the unkempt black or blond hair,
> The ugly legs of the young girls, pistons
> Too powerful for delicacy!
> The women's wrists, the men's arms red
> Used to heat and cold, to toss quartered beeves
> And barrels, and milk-cans, and crates of fruit!
>
> Faces all knotted up like burls on oaks,
> Grasping, fox-snouted, thick-lipped,

> Sagging breasts and protruding stomachs,
> Rasping voices, filthy habits with the hands.
> Nowhere you! Everywhere the electric!
>   (*CEP*, 7)

Here the narrator draws the sharpest possible distinction between his experience of the goddess and his experience of the city dwellers, even though it is clear from his descriptions that they are all equally ugly and equally fascinating.

In the next section, the ambiguity of the goddess increases when she apparently accepts her young disciple's offer of service. From what she says to him, however, it is hard to tell whether she is primarily an external presence or whether she exists also in the minds of the toilers:

> The patch of road between the steep bramble banks;
> The tree in the wind, the white house there, the sky!
> Speak to men of these concerning me!
> For never while you permit them to ignore me
> In these shall the full of my freed voice
> Come grappling the ear with intent!
> Never while the air's clear coolness
> Is seized to be a coat for pettiness;
> Never while richness of greenery
> Stands a shield for prurient minds;
> Never, permitting these things unchallenged
> Shall my voice of leaves and varicolored bark come free
>   through!
>   (*CEP*, 8)

With these words, the goddess seems to confirm the narrator's suspicion that she alone is the principle of the whole world, including of course the world of nature. Indeed, the fact that she is *in* the phenomena as well as transcendent might explain why she keeps turning the narrator around, bringing him back to the world he started from, the world of the city. But, if her omnipresence is genuine, why does he not see her in the toilers? If she really is a universal principle, she ought to be present there as well as in the details

of nature. Oddly enough, the narrator himself seems to grasp this
in a limited way. When he shouts his prophetic warning over the
countryside in compliance with his mentor's request, he describes
the goddess as though she were secretly present in the minds of
those who ignore her:

> Waken! my people, to the boughs green
> With ripening fruit within you!
> Waken to the myriad cinquefoil
> In the waving grass of your minds!
> Waken to the silent phoebe nest
> Under the eaves of your spirit!
>   (CEP, 8)

Unfortunately, nothing happens. With the "weight of the sky"
still upon them, as the goddess puts it, the toilers continue to be
"bowed by their passions / Crushed down" (CEP, 8–9). Perhaps
the warning fails because the narrator has not yet achieved the status of poet, his initiation to poethood still in progress. In any case,
because the goddess herself remains an enigma, her pupil cannot
understand clearly what she requires. In her peculiar "solitude"
(CEP, 8), she is both apart from the world and within it, apart
from the minds of those who ought to be her worshippers and
within them.

In the last section of the poem, the narrator's confused appren-
ticeship ends abruptly with an overwhelming climax. Led to the
edge of the "filthy" Passaic, he is forced to undergo a bizarre ritual
of marriage or baptism, with the goddess officiating:

> Then she, leaping up with a fierce cry:
> "Enter, youth, into this bulk!
> Enter, river, into this young man!"
> Then the river began to enter my heart,
> Eddying back cool and limpid
> Into the crystal beginning of its days.
> But with the rebound it leaped forward:
> Muddy, then black and shrunken
> Till I felt the utter depth of its rottenness

The vile breadth of its degradation
And dropped down knowing this was me now.
But she lifted me and the water took a new tide
Again into the older experiences,
And so, backward and forward,
It tortured itself within me
Until time had been washed finally under,
And the river had found its level
And its last motion had ceased
And I knew all—it became me.
And I knew this for double certain
For there, whitely, I saw myself
Being borne off under the water!
I could have shouted out in my agony
At the sight of myself departing
Forever

(*CEP*, 11–12)

Obviously, the significance of this episode is crucial to any interpretation of the poem as a whole. Before his immersion in the Passaic, the narrator makes the sharpest possible distinction between
the goddess and the city, adoring the one and hating the other. She,
on the other hand, continually frustrates him by sending him back
to the very thing he loathes. Now, at the end of the poem, the goddess purges the narrator of his loathing by forcing him to participate absolutely in the city's "rottenness." It becomes him. But the
question is, to what effect?

The prevailing view seems to be that the narrator is rebuked
for being elitist or escapist. By focusing his attention too narrowly
on the person of the goddess, he has paradoxically ignored the in-
comparable resources of his own urban environment, which, like
everything else, represents one of the goddess's incarnations.
Therefore, he must be humbled or chastened. Breslin reads the final
episode of "The Wanderer" as a dramatic reversal that terminates
the narrator's (hence Williams') "yearning for transcendence."[8]
Likewise, Miller and Riddel see it, in slightly different ways, as an
act of surrender or resignation through which the romantic egoism

of the narrator is simply cancelled or dissolved.[9] Presumably, as an effect of his renovating humiliation, Williams goes off with a new appreciation of things as they are, ready to harmonize himself with the given, whatever it may be. To put it like this, however, would be to give a false impression, or rather a one-sided impression, of an extremely paradoxical situation. Indeed, the narrator of "The Wanderer" *is* purged of his yearning for transcendence, but only because he achieves it. He *does* give up his private consciousness or ego, but only because that ego or consciousness has suddenly expanded to the point where it now contains everything within it. Just as earlier in the poem the goddess seemed to embody the essence of all things, so now, because of his immersion, the narrator himself has become the essence of all things. His wish to be one with the goddess has been granted, though not in the manner he expected, so now he too is the center, the logos. The implications of this become clearer if one considers the similarities between Williams' narrator and Keats's Apollo.

As characters, they resemble each other in several ways. In "The Wanderer," even before his goddess appears to him, the narrator has obscure intimations of the high destiny that awaits him. Later he realizes that his intimations were in fact a preliminary manifestation of the goddess's sacred presence. Thus, in the opening words of the poem, he explains:

> Even in the time when as yet
> I had no certain knowledge of her
> She sprang from the nest, a young crow,
> Whose first flight circled the forest.
> I know now how then she showed me
> Her mind, reaching out to the horizon,
> She close above the tree tops.
> I saw her eyes straining at the new distance
> And as the woods fell from her flying
> Likewise they fell from me as I followed
> So that I strongly guessed all that I must put from me
> To come through ready for the high courses.
>
> (*CEP*, 3)

Similarly, in Book III of "Hyperion," Apollo has intimations of Mnemosyne even before she confronts him directly. Like Williams' goddess, she too is secretly present, sustaining and watching over Apollo on the island of Delos. When at last she does make her appearance, he asks her:

> 'How cam'st thou over the unfooted sea?
> 'Or hath that antique mien and robed form
> 'Mov'd in these vales invisible till now?
> 'Sure I have heard those vestments sweeping o'er
> 'The fallen leaves, when I have sat alone
> 'In cool mid-forest. Surely I have traced
> 'The rustle of those ample skirts about
> 'These grassy solitudes, and seen the flowers
> 'Lift up their heads, as still the whisper pass'd.
> 'Goddess! I have beheld those eyes before,
> 'And their eternal calm, and all that face,
> 'Or I have dream'd.'
>
> ("Hyperion," III, 50–61)[10]

Furthermore, Apollo soon reveals that he too yearns, like the narrator of "The Wanderer," for something higher, something more splendid, than what he has been accustomed to:

> For me, dark, dark,
> 'And painful vile oblivion seals my eyes:
> 'I strive to search wherefore I am so sad,
> 'Until a melancholy numbs my limbs;
> 'And then upon the grass I sit, and moan,
> 'Like one who once had wings. —O why should I
> 'Feel curs'd and thwarted, when the liegeless air
> 'Yields to my step aspirant? Why should I
> 'Spurn the green turf as hateful to my feet?
>
> ("Hyperion," III, 86–94)

Apparently, both Apollo and the narrator of "The Wanderer" feel vaguely entitled to a simple apotheosis with no admixture of pain or suffering. Thus Apollo pleads:

'Goddess benign, point forth some unknown thing:
'Are there not other regions than this isle?
'What are the stars? There is the sun, the sun!
'And the most patient brilliance of the moon!
'And stars by thousands! Point me out the way
'To any one particular beauteous star,
'And I will flit into it with my lyre
'And make its silvery splendour pant with bliss.
                    ("Hyperion," III, 95–102)

If this sounds like something Keats himself might have said in one of his earlier, immature phases, it is clearly beneath the author of "Hyperion." Apollo is not allowed to become a god by avoiding experiences that are "painful" and "vile"; he becomes one by immersing himself in such experiences, albeit vicariously. Indeed, his initiation into the mysteries reflected in Mnemosyne's countenance is accompanied by "wild commotions" not unlike "the struggle at the gate of death":

'Mute thou remainest—mute! yet I can read
'A wondrous lesson in thy silent face:
'Knowledge enormous makes a God of me.
'Names, deeds, grey legends, dire events, rebellions,
'Majesties, sovran voices, agonies,
'Creations and destroyings, all at once
'Pour into the wide hollows of my brain,
'And deify me, as if some blithe wine
'Or bright elixir peerless I had drunk,
'And so become immortal.'
                    ("Hyperion," III, 111–20)

The turmoil that pours into Apollo's brain is, of course, analogous to the river that enters the heart of Williams' wanderer. It is not by flitting away to some beauteous star that Apollo attains his divinity; it is by plunging into the mire of history and experience, which includes not just creations and majesties but also rebellions, agonies, and destroyings. Likewise, the wanderer is so overwhelmed by the river's rottenness that its whole history passes into him. It eddies back into "the crystal beginning of its days," back into "the older experiences," until "time had been washed finally under." If "knowledge enormous" makes a god of Apollo, it has the same effect on the wanderer. "I knew all," he says, "it became me."

But what does it mean to say that William Carlos Williams becomes a god? After all, "The Wanderer" is only an allegory of Williams' development as a poet. But "Hyperion" too is just such an allegory as Keats himself makes clear in his revision of it. In "The Fall of Hyperion," the vision formerly granted to Apollo is given to the narrator. It is the narrator, therefore, not Apollo, who tells us in the second version that, as a result of his encounter with Moneta,

> there grew
> A power within me of enormous ken
> To see as a god sees, and take the depth
> Of things as nimbly as the outward eye
> Can size and shape pervade.
> ("The Fall of Hyperion," I, 302–06)

What is this "knowledge enormous," this "power . . . of enormous ken" that both Keats and Williams desire and even claim for themselves as the indispensable quality of a true poet? It has to do, I think, with the achievement of a standpoint outside the normal course of experience. Only from such a standpoint—outside of, or independent of, ordinary experience—can experience itself be contemplated as a whole. Naturally, this involves a certain renunciation of self, but the self renounced is merely the finite self, the delimited, servile consciousness of the ordinary man or woman. In recompense for the renunciation of this ordinary self, the poet gains access to many selves, in fact to the whole range of human experience. If Keats passes easily from Iago to Imogen or from Imogen to a sparrow picking about in the gravel outside his window, or from all three to the individual identities of a whole room full of people, it is because he himself has no particular character, unlike everything and everyone else he encounters, and is engaged in no particular activity other than that of pure contemplation—

when he is being a poet. This power of transcendence is precisely what makes possible his celebrated empathy. Being, as it were, on the outside of everything, he can look into anything with an intensity that an ordinary involvement with the thing would preclude.[11]

By the same token, Apollo in "Hyperion" does not participate in events in the same way the Titans do. They pass from virtually unruffled sovereignty to a condition of painful, almost human limitation without being able to grasp what has happened to them. With the possible exception of Oceanus (who knows that "to bear all naked truths, / And to envisage circumstance, all calm, / . . . is the top of sovereignty"), the Titans are completely dismayed by the course of events which has them in its grip. They are like members of an audience watching a play who suddenly find themselves precipitated into the action of the play as characters. Apollo, on the other hand, transcends what happens to the Titans by knowing it instantaneously and vicariously. When he looks at Mnemosyne's face, he sees the entire panorama of history (including, presumably, the fall of the Titans) "all at once." In that moment, he is necessarily superior to that which he beholds. He moves, so to speak, outside the poem, which explains why the poem breaks off as it does. If after his apotheosis Apollo were allowed to enter into the main action on the same level as the other characters, if he were allowed to become involved, for example, in some sort of epic contest with Hyperion, he would in a sense forfeit the "knowledge enormous" that is the very basis of his divinity. Instead of being outside the whole engaged in an act of contemplation that assimilates everything, he would be a part of the whole and thus considerably diminished. Instead of having a vision of the whole, he would be merely an element of that which is envisioned. Undoubtedly, Keats himself realized this, for, when he came to revise the poem, he insured the preservation of Apollo's transcendent standpoint by giving it over to the narrator. (In its own way, of course, this maneuver is every bit as momentous as the overthrow of the Titans in "Hyperion," to which it is analogous: the gods themselves are eclipsed by the consciousness that has the power to conceive of them, that is to say, by the poet's imaginative power.) After his

initiation, the narrator of "The Fall of Hyperion" becomes virtually a pure consciousness, witnessing events but not participating
in them. Once again, however, the poem breaks off, this time fore-
shortened by the obsolescence of its own mythological material.

If in one sense Apollo is detached from events, in another sense
he is even closer to them than the Titans are. When the panorama
of experience pours into the "wide hollows" of his brain, it "becomes" him in the same way that the "all" becomes Williams' wanderer. Henceforth, there is nothing that can be said to exist apart
from Apollo's consciousness of it. In fact, the meaning or significance of each event, each object, resides only there, for only there
can it be said to be properly apprehended. This, I think, is precisely
the implication of "The Wanderer." If it is correct at all to speak
of a merger in that poem between subject and object, of a unity or
a harmony established between Williams and his world, it is simply because, like Apollo, Williams has drawn all things into himself. As the "all" enters his mind, it becomes his idea, while he, on
the other hand, becomes the single, transcendent point of unity—
the *logos*, the center, the coherence. Indeed, on the evidence of this
first major poem it might well be said that, instead of abandoning
idealism, Williams actually embraces it.[12]

Fortunately, we do not have to depend entirely on "The Wanderer" to see where Williams was headed at this point in his development. A year after the poem appeared in *The Egoist*, Williams
wrote a wonderfully revealing essay called "Vortex," which has
only recently been published in Bram Dijkstra's collection *A Recognizable Image*. This essay, which takes romantic egoism even
further than the essay by Gaudier-Brzeska that occasioned Williams' piece, shows quite clearly that Williams refused to humble
himself in the presence of "facts" or "things" and, consequently,
did not develop a deferential attitude toward his environment.[13]
On the contrary, the central theme of Williams' essay is that he has
the right to use anything whatsoever for the purpose of self-expression without compromising himself or impairing his independence
in any way. Instead of asking, as the wanderer does prior to his initiation, "How shall I be a mirror to this modernity?" Williams asks,

in effect, "How shall this modernity be a mirror to me?" Or rather, he simply declares as an axiom that everything he touches must of necessity reflect him. This is not an abandonment of the ego; it is an affirmation of it. Significantly, "Vortex" opens with the words "I affirm my existence" and ends very nearly with the words "I affirm my independence." Whatever its circumstances and whatever those circumstances appear to dictate, the ego remains perfectly unconstrained. "Thus," says Williams,

by accepting the opportunity that has best satisfied my desire to express my emotions in the environment in which I have happened to be, I have defied my environment and denied its power to control me or [the power] of any accident that has made me write instead of cut stone.

By taking whatever character my environment has presented and turning it to my purpose, I have expressed my independence of it. (*ARI*, 58)

The moment Williams refuses to acknowledge the authority over him of "fact" or "thing," the world, and everything in it, becomes, at least potentially, an extension or projection of his ego. This is not a denial of idealism; it *is* idealism. For now it is not the ego that depends on the environment but the environment that depends on the ego. Thus Williams writes in his essay on Byron Vazakas: "No world can exist for more than the consuming of a match or the eating of an apple without a poet to breathe into it an immortality."[14] Once he has grasped this fact, the whole world becomes for Williams an objective correlative. He becomes its significance, which is why he can say with perfect confidence:

I will express my emotions in the appearances: surfaces, sounds, smells, touch of the place in which I happen to be.

I will not make an effort to leave that place for I deny that I am dependent on any place. (*ARI*, 58)

In one sense, of course, Williams needs appearances, for they are the means whereby he comes to know himself: "by appearances I know my emotion" (*ARI*, 57). In another sense, though, he does not need them, or rather he needs to be able to reject them. To preserve its essential transcendence, the ego must be free not only to take whatever appearance fits its purpose but also to express whatever emotion happens to occur. By exercising its freedom, it distinguishes itself from its own manifestations—from all appearances and all emotions. Hence Williams concludes: "I affirm my independence of all emotions and my denial in time and place of the accident of their appearance" (*ARI*, 58–59).

One reason why "Vortex" is so important is that it constitutes the first explicit statement of a paradox that is implicit in "The Wanderer" and central to Williams' work as a whole. On the one hand, when everything becomes a part of Williams' mind, the entire phenomenal world becomes available to him as a means of self-expression. All of that world becomes intensely interesting and worthy of the most careful inspection, because it all lies within the scope of Williams' power and is capable of reflecting back to him the depths of his own mind. On the other hand, in contemplating the nature of its own transcendence, the ego must also insist that nothing in the phenomenal world is really adequate to represent that which exceeds all phenomena—namely, itself. In some sense, therefore, the phenomenal world must be transcended or used in such a way that it points beyond itself. This paradox wherein the phenomenal world is both affirmed and negated is inherent not only in Williams' work but in romantic poetry generally. Indeed, in the final analysis, Keatsian empathy and Wordsworthian egotism, both of which are present in Williams, seem almost indistinguishable, each presupposing the other as its own unspoken foundation.

That Williams' inclination toward idealism was not a passing thing will become increasingly evident in the course of the present study. For the moment, though, a glance at some of his later writing may suggest how relentlessly he pursued its implications. For example, in *The Embodiment of Knowledge*, written during the late 1920s, Williams reiterates again and again that nothing we claim as part of our experience exists in itself apart from our perception of it:

Well, what does one see? to paint? Why the tree, of course, is the facile answer. Not at all. The tree as a tree does not exist literally, figuratively or any way you please—for the appraising eye of the artist—or any man—the tree does not exist. What does exist, and in heightened intensity for the artist is the impression created by the shape and color of an object before him in his sensual being—his whole body (not his eyes) his body, his mind, his memory, his place: himself—that is what he sees—And in America—escape it he cannot—it is an American tree.

Render that in pigment and he asserts his own existence and that of men about him—he becomes prophet and seer—in so far as he is wholly worthy to be so. (*EK*, 24–25)

The primary value of a work of art is that it reveals a truth applicable to all human perception, namely, that perception is creative or constitutive. If, as Williams often claims, a poem or a painting has the same ontological status as any other object in the world, it is only because all objects, as objects, are equally dependent on the mind that perceives them. The words of a poem, the stars in the heavens—"are they not," asks Williams, "corollaries only of the brain? Were we to scrape the words from the paper, or the stars from the sky, they would mean alike, nothing. It is only in their interrelationship with the perceptions that we know them. And there they are equally real" (*EK*, 128). In the same way, science, poetry, and philosophy are equally valuable (or equally trivial) in the sense that they are really "no more than material manifestations" of the human brain (*EK*, 130). If Williams tends to value poetry and the other arts more than science and philosophy, he does so because, in his view, the results of science and philosophy are usually mistaken for objective truths independent of the minds that think them. A painting or a poem, however, is manifestly the creation of the mind that produces it, and so, by its very existence, it proclaims a truth which the superstructures of science and philosophy tend to make us forget.

In most forms of idealism, it is only a short step from the notion that reality is dependent on the mind to the more radical notion that the mind itself is the ultimate object of knowledge. The egoism of "Vortex" suggests that Williams took this step at the very beginning of his career. However, the clearest expression of the consequences of idealism, as far as Williams is concerned, may be found in the following remark to John C. Thirlwall, which was written in 1955:

The mind always tries to break out of confinement. It has tried every sort of interest which presents itself, even to a flight to the moon. But the only thing which will finally interest it must be its own intrinsic nature. In itself it must find devices which will permit it to survive—physical transportation to another planet will not help, for it will still be the same mind which has not been relieved by movement. (*SL*, 330–31)

This passage shows us that the merger of mind and world depicted in "The Wanderer" may eventually lead, and in Williams' case did lead, to the higher recognition that mind itself is the ultimate object of knowledge. If the phenomenal world is really epiphenomenal with respect to mind, empathy plays into or gives way to the egotistical sublime. Thus, when Williams tells us in one of his late essays that art raises "the dignity of man" by allowing him "to say, *I am*, in concrete terms" (*ARI*, 212), or when he exclaims at the end of "The Desert Music," "I *am* a poet! I / am. I am" (*PB*, 120), he is simply reaffirming what Coleridge asserts in the *Biographia Literaria* to be the one basic principle of knowledge, namely, the mind's intrinsic spiritual power:

This principle . . . manifests itself in the SUM or I AM, which I shall hereafter indiscriminately express by the words spirit, self and selfconsciousness. In this, and in this alone, object and subject, being and knowing, are identical, each involving and supposing the other. In other words, it is a subject which becomes a subject by the act of constructing itself objectively to itself; but which is never an object except for itself, and only so far as by the very same act it becomes a subject.[15]

For Coleridge, as for Williams, the identity of subject and object is not to be thought of as a union or harmony of two essentially different things. It is to be thought of as the identity of one thing with itself, as the self-identity of mind or spirit. As Coleridge expresses it, a spirit, by its very definition, is "self-representative"; it has (or rather it is) the power by which it comes to know itself. But it exercises this power only by constructing itself in opposition to itself as an object for itself. Since this is what a spirit must do in order to be a spirit, it follows, according to Coleridge, that "the spirit in all the objects which it views, views only itself."

What happens then, however? What happens after the spirit becomes aware that its acts of consciousness are really acts of selfconsciousness, after the mind discovers that "the only thing which will finally interest it must be its own intrinsic nature"? A withdrawal of some sort usually occurs as the mind or spirit, returning to itself, abandons the objects it has used as the vehicles of its self-awareness. In romantic poetry, this withdrawal is often painful and depressing, but it may also be the prelude to an insight that transcends pain and depression. It is certainly painful when Coleridge observes in his "Dejection Ode" that he may not hope "from outward forms to win / The passion and the life, whose fountains are within"—painful because it means that nature cannot henceforth be regarded as a truly companionable form. Apart from the animating spirit of Coleridge himself, nature is merely object, and as an object it is "dead, fixed, incapable in itself of any action, and necessarily finite."[16] Likewise, it is painful when Wordsworth in Book VI of *The Prelude* observes the difference between "a living thought" of Mount Blanc and the "soulless image on the eye" produced by the actual mountain. In each of these examples, the impulse to celebrate "the one Life within us and abroad" or "the something far more deeply interfused" is superseded by the awareness of a fundamental distinction that has to be made between spirit and matter or mind and nature. A possible consequence of this awareness may be the stoical humanism of Wordsworth's "Elegiac Stanzas" or Arnold's "Dover Beach." However, another, more positive consequence may be that in coming to know itself, the mind may also come to know the nature of mind in general or the nature of the one mind, which is God. Through an act of reflection, "the conditional finite I" (to use Coleridge's terms) may learn to see itself as dependent on, or inherent in, "the absolute I AM." "We begin," says Coleridge, "with the I KNOW MYSELF, in order to end with the absolute I AM. We proceed from the self, in order to lose and find all self in God."[17] Similarly, Wordsworth's temporarily disabling discovery of the inadequacy of "the soulless image on the eye" by comparison with the "living thought" makes possible the higher intuition that "Our destiny, our nature, and our home / Is with infinitude, and only there." Thus, by a circuitous route, both Coleridge and Wordsworth trace their way back into the fold of religious orthodoxy.

Williams' case, I would argue, is only slightly different from theirs. While it is true that he never had much use for "religion" in the usual sense, being convinced that the genuine "immanence of a religious experience" (*SE*, 215) is necessarily perverted by institutions, nevertheless he did come to believe in the existence of something like a universal spirit or a universal mind in which all finite minds necessarily participate. Though he generally shied away from using terms like "God," he was still impelled to acknowledge the ultimate source of his own creative power in language unmistakably associated with religious mysticism. In his *Autobiography*, he calls it "the secret spring of all our lives" (*A*, 359). Elsewhere he calls it "the Unknown," "the living flame," the "radiant gist," "the mystery about which nothing can be said." Like Coleridge and Wordsworth, he is led from a consideration of his own transcendence of phenomena to a consideration of Transcendence itself conceived of as a single, ineffable spiritual power.[18]

Williams' idealism, then, is paradoxical because it implies not only the most intimate connection but also the most severe disjunction between Williams himself and the phenomenal world. This paradox, as I have said, is not unique to Williams—it is characteristic of romantic poetry generally. The romantic poet is typically drawn in two different directions. On the one hand, he is enticed into the world of the senses, to "the mighty world / Of eye, and ear," to "this goodly universe," which is usually called "Nature." On the other hand, he is equally attracted to what Wordsworth calls "the invisible world," which is not available to the gross, bodily eye but only to the "inward eye" of contemplation. Thus for every passage that celebrates a harmonious interrelationship, "an ennobling interchange," between the poet's mind and the "external" world, there is a counterpassage somewhere that celebrates the preeminence of mind over world. For every acknowledgment of "the one Life within us and abroad," there is also a recognition that the mind of man is, as Wordsworth says, "A thousand times more beautiful than the earth / On which he dwells."

One way to explain this paradox would be to remember that, from the point of view of idealism, the poet's mind—indeed any

mind—is related to the world in the same way that God, in traditional terms, is related to the Creation. Coleridge, for example, defines the "primary" imagination, which is the prototype of the
"secondary" or "poetical" imagination, as itself "a repetition in the
finite mind of the eternal act of creation in the infinite I AM."[19] By
the same token, Emerson considers man "the creator in the finite"
(CW, I, 38), since the natural world is not so much built up around
him as it is put forth through him. It follows that the poet, like
God, is both transcendent and immanent, not only with respect to
the world of the secondary imagination but also with respect to
the world of the primary imagination. The need to express both
sides of this complex relationship, that is to say, both transcendence
and immanence, accounts for the typically romantic oscillation between egotism and empathy.

Nevertheless, while it is impossible to think of the world in idealistic terms as truly external or independent of the mind that thinks
it,[20] it is indeed possible and even necessary in some forms of idealism to think of the mind as something superior to, or independent
of, its own particular manifestations. And this means that, in one
way or another, the concept of transcendence supersedes that of
immanence.[21] Accordingly, if we look closely at Williams' work,
we find that it embodies a spiritual drama wherein the mind comes
to an understanding of itself by using the phenomenal world of appearances as a means of achieving self-awareness. In doing this, his
work conforms not only to Coleridge's formulas in the Biographia
but also to the fundamental principles of aesthetics according to
Hegel, the greatest of all modern idealists.

Hegel's lectures on the philosophy of fine art or aesthetics, which
were delivered in Berlin during the 1820s, revolve around the very
paradox we have just been considering. For Hegel, art is supremely
valuable because it represents a fusion of that which is spiritual or
universal with that which is sensuous or particular. On one level art
is a manifestation of the human spirit, so that our need for art may
be defined as "man's rational need to lift the inner and outer world
into his spiritual consciousness as an object in which he recognizes
again his own self."[22] Simultaneously, on another level, art is one

of the means whereby the Absolute spirit constructs itself objectively to itself in order to know itself. In Hegel's words:

The spirit in its truth is absolute. Therefore it is not an essence lying in abstraction beyond the objective world. On the contrary, it is present within objectivity in the finite spirit's recollection or inwardization of the essence of all things—i.e. the finite apprehends itself in its own essence and so itself becomes essential and absolute.[23]

The first form this apprehension takes is the form of art, which Hegel describes as "an immediate and therefore *sensuous* knowing, a knowing, in the form and shape of the sensuous and objective itself, in which the Absolute is presented to contemplation and feeling."[24] Indeed, Hegel even claims at one point that "when art is present in its supreme perfection, then precisely in its figurative mode [that is to say, the mode of sensuous configuration] it contains the kind of exposition most essential to and most in correspondence with the content of truth."[25] In this respect, art has a dignity comparable to that of religion and philosophy, a dignity that Hegel manifestly acknowledges by devoting himself to an exhaustive survey of the history of art in all its forms and phases.

Nevertheless, for all his insistence that works of art have a spiritual content, being sensuous manifestations of the Absolute, Hegel also declares, without the slightest sense of having contradicted himself, that "the manifestation of truth in a sensuous form is not truly adequate to the spirit."[26] Art is merely the first of three stages in the development of the Absolute's understanding of itself. The second and third stages, which transcend the first, are, respectively, those associated with religion and philosophy. Hegel, as a philosopher, necessarily considers himself to have reached a point of contemplation from which it is possible to see that art has already completed its own course of development and has therefore become obsolete:

For us art counts no longer as the highest mode in which truth fashions an existence for itself. In general it was early in history that thought passed judgement against art as a mode of illustrating the idea of the Divine; this happened with the Jews and Mohammedans, for example, and indeed even with the Greeks, for Plato opposed the gods of Homer

and Hesiod starkly enough. With the advance of civilization a time generally comes in the case of every people when art points beyond itself.
For example, the historical elements in Christianity, the Incarnation of
Christ, his life and death, have given to art, especially painting, all sorts
of opportunities for development, and the Church itself has nursed art
or let it alone; but when the urge for knowledge and research, and the
need for inner spirituality, instigated the Reformation, religious ideas
were drawn away from their wrapping in the element of sense and
brought back to the inwardness of heart and thinking. Thus the *'after'*
of art consists in the fact that there dwells in the spirit the need to satisfy
itself solely in its own inner self as the true form for truth to take. Art
in its beginnings still leaves over something mysterious, a secret forebod-
ing and a longing, because its creations have not completely set forth
their full content for imaginative vision. But if the perfect content has
been perfectly revealed in artistic shapes, then the more far-seeing spirit
rejects this objective manifestation and turns back into its inner self.
This is the case in our own time. We may well hope that art will always
rise higher and come to perfection, but the form of art has ceased to be
the supreme need of the spirit.[27]

Hegel makes it clear in this passage that, while art must always in
some sense represent the spiritual in the form of the sensuous, it
"points beyond itself" in that it leads eventually to an awareness
of the spirit's transcendence of the sensuous.

Hegel's resolution of the paradox that art both succeeds and fails
in expressing a spiritual content is based on the supposition that art
waxes and wanes in three successive stages. In the first stage, which
Hegel calls "the symbolic," the spirit seeks embodiment in sensuous form, but fails because it has not yet attained a sufficient degree
of self-awareness. It embodies itself inappropriately in forms that
can only be described as grotesque or ridiculous, as Hegel tries to
demonstrate with examples from oriental or Eastern art. In the
second stage, which he calls "the classical," the spirit succeeds in
achieving a perfect embodiment of itself in the architectural and,
principally, the sculptural representations of the ancient Greeks.
In the third and final stage, however, the so-called "romantic" stage
(under which term Hegel includes practically all Western art since
the dawn of the Christian era), the spirit achieves such a high degree of self-awareness that it eventually recognizes the inadequacy
of its own sensuous manifestations. As Hegel explains, "at the stage

of romantic art the spirit knows that its truth does not consist in its immersion in corporeality; on the contrary, it only becomes sure of its truth by withdrawing from the external into its own intimacy with itself and positing external reality as an existence inadequate to itself."[28] For this reason, says Hegel, "the true content of romantic art is absolute inwardness, and its corresponding form is spiritual subjectivity with its grasp of its independence and freedom."[29] The fact that the romantic artist must use sensuous materials to express this content suggests that art has indeed turned against itself or pointed beyond itself in a way that precludes further development. If all art is inherently paradoxical, nevertheless it is in the third and final stage of its development that the paradox becomes conspicuous, for, as Hegel defines it, "romantic art is the self-transcendence of art but within its own sphere and in the form of art itself."[30]

If Hegel, though, is relevant to an understanding of Williams, it is not simply because both are idealists and are therefore obliged to contemplate the same paradoxical relationship between spirit and matter or mind and world. It is because, in his own relatively limited way, like an embryo recapitulating the evolutionary process in the womb, Williams recapitulates the entire three-stage process whereby art as a whole develops, according to Hegel.[31] Like the symbolic artist, for example, Williams experiences the origin of art in terms of a desire or a need to establish, via formal expression, a harmony between himself and the world to which he stands opposed. As he explains in one of the prose passages in *Spring and All:* "The inevitable flux of the seeing eye toward measuring itself by the world it inhabits can only result in . . . crushing humiliation unless the individual raise to some approximate co-extension with the universe" (*I*, 105). Furthermore, in acknowledging as he often does that his poems may very well fail to achieve the desired clarity or fullness of expression, Williams seems to offer a description of his work which corresponds to Hegel's description of symbolic art as a mere approximation of that which it seeks to express. Thus, in a letter written in 1913 to Harriet Monroe, Williams observes:

To tell the truth, I myself never quite feel that I know what I am talking about—if I did, and when I do, the thing written seems nothing to me. However, what I do write and allow to survive I always feel is mighty worth while and that nobody else has ever come as near as I have to the thing I have intimated if not expressed. To me it's a matter of first understanding that which may not yet be put to words. I might add more but to no purpose. In a sense, I must express myself, you're right, but always completely incomplete if that means anything. (*SL*, 26)

Nearly forty years later, Williams reiterated this attitude toward his art in a letter to Henry Wells in which he defined the poem in general (though *Paterson*, in particular, was the poem on his mind) as "an attempt, an experiment, a failing experiment, toward assertion with broken means" (*SL*, 286). To the extent that he actually cultivates such a conception, Williams appears to endorse the imperfection that Hegel describes as the essence of "symbolism."

At the same time, however, we know that Williams did aspire all his life to achieve the kind of perfect expression which Hegel ascribes only to classical art and that he thought he could do so by inventing a strictly formal pattern which might be regarded as the sensuous equivalent of his otherwise imperceptible, incoherent feelings. "In art," he wrote in 1928, "not only is a full statement permissible . . . a complete statement is compulsory" (*ARI*, 73), provided it be understood that such a statement is to be made "strictly in the realm of art, that is pure form." If, after all, a poem is truly "a mechanism that has a function which is to say something as accurately and as clearly as possible,"[32] it follows that expression may be simply a matter of mechanics, a matter of verbal engineering. Like others of his generation, Williams appears to have felt, at least part of the time, that technical experimentation might be the key to unprecedented triumphs of artistic expression, making art once more the supreme achievement of the human spirit Hegel considered it to have been during the golden age of Greece. Thus with an air of confidence Williams declares: "When the poem has achieved its particular form unlike any other, when it shall stand alone—then we have achieved our language. We have said what it is in our minds to say."[33]

All the more depressing, then, when at last it becomes clear that we can never say what it is in our minds to say? Not in the least. For it is precisely this failure, which Williams acknowledges repeatedly throughout his long career, that becomes the real triumph. It becomes a triumph as soon as Williams realizes that it signifies that the power within him, which he has it in his mind to say, sublimely exceeds every possible manifestation and, therefore, every possible artistic form. As soon as he realizes that the function of art is to bear witness to a spiritual source with which the work of art itself can never coincide and to which all art must be forever incommensurate, Williams achieves a degree of self-awareness that, according to Hegel, is characteristic only of the last and highest phase of art, the romantic. Although it is difficult to say exactly when Williams achieves this awareness, it appears that he had a romantic conception of art, in Hegel's sense, almost from the very start, as is evident from the explicit egoism of "Vortex." If this is true, then the presence in Williams' work of attitudes that correspond more closely to what Hegel describes as the symbolic and the classical phases of art may be explained by the fact that even romantic art is still art. The romantic artist, to the degree that he *is* an artist and not a philosopher, experiences both the need to express himself in sensuous forms and the confidence as well that his expressions can be truly adequate. If, as Hegel says, romantic art is the self-transcendence of art, it is so only "within its own sphere and in the form of art itself." In fact, as we pursue our investigation of Williams, we shall find that he was constantly striving *within his art* to express the nature of his own spiritual preeminence, not only with respect to the world of natural phenomena, but also with respect to art itself. For this reason alone, he must be considered primarily "romantic" in the Hegelian sense of the term.

However, the interrelationship of failure and success in Williams' poetics is scarcely intelligible—nor is his idealism as a whole intelligible—without at least some reference to his own, unique version of the myth of the fall. We must pause, therefore, to consider the outlines of this myth before proceeding further.

2 Williams' Version of the Myth of the Fall and the Problem of Symbols

A fall of some sort or other—the creation, as it were, of the non-absolute—is the fundamental postulate of the moral history of man. Without this hypothesis, man is unintelligible; with it, every phenomenon is explicable. The mystery itself is too profound for human insight.

—COLERIDGE, *Table Talk,* 1 May 1830

For all their significance, neither "Vortex" nor "The Wanderer" is the most revealing of Williams' early texts. That distinction belongs, I would argue, to the fourth essay in a group of "Five Philosophical Essays" written by Williams sometime between 1910 and 1915. Although he never published any of these essays, the fourth, entitled "Love and Service," happens to be the clearest and most comprehensive explanation Williams ever wrote of what his work as a whole is all about. Reading it, we learn how deeply committed he was to a certain conception of the fall and how much that conception influenced his adoption of the epistemology and aesthetics of idealism. As a result, the rationale behind Williams' poetry, so often misconstrued in the past, becomes finally clear.

The essay begins boldly with the assertion that perception, and perception alone, constitutes the whole duty of man. We start with perception and end with perception, though, as we shall see presently, both our starting point and our end point are curiously elusive. By comparison to what Williams regards as the most important activity of man, which is to admire everything that exists, the activities whereby we acquire formal knowledge, like the more practical activities of "routine life" whereby we insure our material existence, are trivial and irrelevant:

AS FAR AS any ultimate problem of the universe is concerned man on earth must forever be totally ignorant. For him all simply exists. He cannot know anything; he cannot even begin to know; he can merely appreciate; his sole possible activity can be but of two orders: to behold and to behold more. The why is unthinkable and action and will are merely corollaries of sight, not separate. Man is to thrill as the great horses of existence prance by him, he being one of them also, and to keep from being stepped on by knowing where the hoof will fall next. His only actions are to prance to cheer and to point, all of which are but one thing: praise. (*EK*, 178)

"Thus," says Williams, "we live and eat merely to go about in the face of wonder in the fullest glory of our senses only differing from infants in a breadth of accomplishment and expression" (*EK*, 180–81). The act of pure appreciation can be called a starting point because, according to Williams, it is especially characteristic of the

consciousness of children ("infants") and primitives. At the same
time, however, it must also be called an end point or a goal, because
it represents the "consummation" of life's "essential spirit" (*EK*,
180). Even for the most sophisticated adult, the whole meaning of
life remains concentrated in "moments of intense feeling" that are
occasioned by perceptions and devoted entirely to praise and appreciation.

The trouble is that we have left our starting point behind; we
have become sophisticated. When the activity of pure appreciation
is eclipsed by other activities, as it surely is both in the life of the
individual and in the life of the race, a fall occurs. As soon as he
eats of the tree of knowledge, man starts building the edifices of
science and philosophy, and simultaneously he begins to lose his
capacity for wonder. Instead of devoting himself naïvely and directly to the mystery of existence, he starts to explain the mystery
and thence becomes distracted by his own explanations. The result
is a form of sophisticated idolatry so abhorrent to Williams that he
launches into a passionate defense of what he takes to be its opposite, namely, the unsophisticated worship of primitives:

> That native was no fool who first praised the sun and the moon. We
> too shall have moon and sun feasts; we shall come to realize much that
> we now do not understand. Call this native an idolater, call him what
> you will. What is the moon to him? It is a light, a sign. He doesn't even
> know it is round. To him it is merely wonder, the unknown that is
> beautiful; to him it is an unconscious symbol which he used for praise.
> His, until perversion sets in through ignorance, is true expression, but
> you, you can see nothing but a dead sphere of clay which is not even
> true vision but half superstitious fancy, but the native sees beauty,
> wonder! You are the fool, not he. Or else what do you do that is better
> if you will not be called a fool? You have no beauty your own nor
> even a symbol of beauty except dead words, though there are many live
> ones, dead words which are symbols of symbols, twice removed from
> vitality—on a string like dried apples or Swedish bread. You are the
> idolaters, not the native. Oh you hypocrites, you shall yet kneel to the
> sun and moon and be cleaned. (*EK*, 181)

The difference between the native and ourselves is this: whereas
the native uses that which he sees as a symbol, we mistake our symbols for that which we see. The native is not an idolater (not, that

is, "until perversion sets in through ignorance") because he does not worship the sun and moon in and for themselves. Rather he expresses, by means of his praise of the sun and the moon, what Williams regards as a properly worshipful attitude toward that which transcends all symbols, namely, "the unknown" or "the mystery about which nothing can be said" (*EK*, 182). Since this alone is the real object of his praise, his use of the sun and moon as vehicles of praise constitutes "true expression," not idolatry. We, on the other hand, *are* idolaters, though not because we use symbols. We are idolaters because the symbols we use do not point directly to the mystery. Instead, they point to other symbols. As Williams puts it, they are "symbols of symbols." What he means by this, I think, is that we no longer apprehend the world of the senses as a symbol of the unknown—instead we apprehend it as an object of knowledge. Accordingly, we have developed increasingly complex systems of explanation that refer to the world as though it were a thing in itself, the terminus of all explanation. As these systems grow in complexity, they eventually interfere with our awareness of the things they are supposed to explain, so that, if we are not careful, we find ourselves attending exclusively to representations of things that are themselves representations of the unknown, or "symbols of symbols." Instead of remaining awed by the ineffable mystery of existence, we substitute in the most complacent and idolatrous fashion our own conceptions for that which is ultimately inconceivable. This is what Williams means by the fall.

But the fall is more than just an accidental by-product of personal or cultural development. It is the inevitable consequence of every act of expression that attends every act of perception. No matter how pure it is in its origin, every attempt to give shape or form to one's admiration of the mystery of existence involves the use of symbols, and when these symbols are confused with the reality they stand for, the fall occurs. In a way, then, the fall is as much the result of a misapprehension of works of art as it is the result of science and philosophy. Even the native's "true expression" is potentially idolatrous, as Williams admits when he refers to the apparently inevitable moment "when perversion sets in through ignorance." The fall, therefore, is not to be interpreted as an event that occurs once and for all in the history of a culture or in the history of an individual. It is, so to speak, an eternal event, an ongoing event, constantly repeated, whose necessity springs, oddly enough, from the very mystery that excites our admiration and compels our praise.

We may say, in fact, that the fall occurs because, as Williams describes it, the act of perception leads naturally and inevitably to expression, and the act of expression is always, in some sense, a misrepresentation. What happens during one of those moments of pure appreciation when no distraction separates a man from his sense of the mystery? Williams tells us:

He finds no use for any formality he practices by habit, all he knows how to do is mechanically rejected by his mind until at last he is totally powerless in speech and limb, his whole being given to sight, to appreciation. Then comes a miracle, he has no satisfaction in his learned activities so at once he invents something new. He tries to sing, he tries to dance, to speak praises in accordance with that which he sees but, of course, fails. The point however is that he tried to do a thing which had he been able he would have done and that thing was to perform some act which would symbolize the beauty he sees, reflect it and this is expression, the outgrowth of sight, an act of appreciation, praise. One wishes to be a poet, a painter, a something instinctively known to be supreme, a something of which the essence is sight in the broad sense, to include hearing, but the reality he would express is silence. (*EK*, 180)

Being "outgrowths" of sight, all forms of expression can be said to have as their ultimate ground those acts of pure perception that constitute the fruit of our immediate contact with the world. Nevertheless, since the real object of our perceptions is the unknown "about which nothing can be said," every attempt to express this real object must fail. Since the reality we would express is "silence," every speaking is necessarily not in accordance with that which prompts us to speak. And yet, Williams insists, "we must seek for forms by which to express, for we cannot, except in silence, praise direct, it must take a form and that form is beauty" (*EK*, 181).

The artist, it seems, no less than the philosopher or the scientist, creates misrepresentations of reality. Even his work is the symbol of a symbol in the sense that the beauty he makes is merely a symbol of the beauty he sees and that beauty, in turn, is a symbol of that which is formless and ineffable. On the other hand, he cannot be silent without, in a way, betraying his perception, for it is the perception itself that impels him to speak. Another, more pressing reason for not remaining silent has to do with the fact that previous expressions of all sorts are constantly interfering with new acts of appreciation and must, therefore, be destroyed. In order to liberate himself and others from the powerful charm exerted by these distractions, the artist must make a positive gesture to cancel or negate them. Finding himself surrounded by symbols and knowing the difference between symbols and the reality beyond symbols, he must demonstrate the difference and abolish idolatry by using symbols in such a way as to reveal that they are just that—mere symbols. Furthermore, he must do this not only with the symbols of his art, with paint or words or tones, but also with the "natural" symbols of his experience, with the things he encounters in daily life:

> But two things we must avoid. We must not forget that we praise the unknown, the mystery about which nothing can be said; and second, that we praise in silence, the rest being but perishable signs. Then lest we mistake our signs for the reality let them be ever new, forever new for only by forever changing the sign can we learn to separate from it its meaning, the expression from the term, and so cease to be idolaters.
>
> For I could live forever in a hut in a valley and if I were born there I would mistake the valley for peace, the hut for comfort, my dog for love, one flower for beauty and myself for king of creation just as has been done many times in the past. Therefore I travel. Manners that differ, customs, worships that differ show that no language, no custom, no worship is the truth but the truth is a formless thing which lies in them as within a suit of clothes, in part. Then I see that I must be forever new lest I become an idolater in my valley, but I would be the biggest fool imaginable if I took my valley to express nothing. (*EK*, 182)

These remarks make it plain beyond a doubt that Williams' notorious iconoclasm is, above all, conservative.[1] It seeks to conserve, not to destroy, what it takes to be an original intuition of the ultimate ground of our existence—the formless truth. When the icon is smashed, when the symbol is allowed to perish, then that which stands above icons and symbols may be apprehended as utterly transcendent. Or, to use Williams' terms, "when the form is destroyed the permanent shines out for the first time clearly" (*EK*, 185). Here we see a corroboration of Emerson's paradoxical observation that "the spiritualist finds himself driven to express his faith by a series of skepticisms" (*CE*, IV, 181).

In "Love and Service," however, Williams does not hesitate, as he does almost everywhere else, to express his faith openly and directly. With prophetic fervor he declares that "men shall come to the great altar of the Unknown with pomp and singing and processions" (*EK*, 181), thereby cancelling the idolatry into which they have fallen. When this happens, we shall have come in one sense full circle, for we shall have regained that original apprehension of the unknown which Williams supposes to have flourished prior to the perversions of sophistication. In the beginning, apparently, this apprehension was facilitated by the use of "unconscious symbols." In the end, it will be facilitated by the highly conscious process of using symbols to displace symbols. Thus, in another sense, we shall have risen from a lower plane to a higher. Starting with a naïve affirmation of particular symbols (the valley standing for peace, the hut for comfort, the dog for love, etc.), we end by rejecting such symbols as inadequate manifestations of the formless truth.

But what, after all, is this truth? What is this mystery about which nothing can be said except that it is "the Unknown"? The title of Williams' essay, "Love and Service," comes as near as possible to providing an answer, because love and service as Williams describes them constitute the most significant expressions in human experience of what the mystery means. Indeed, the relationship that exists between love in its essence, or love in itself, and a pair of human lovers is exactly the same as the relationship that exists between the formless truth and the perishable forms. "Love," therefore, is one of the primary names Williams gives to the unknown, without intending thereby to diminish its ineffability, for the effect of using such a name is not so much to clarify the mystery as it is to make love itself, as we normally understand it, even more mysterious.[2] When two human beings love each other, says Williams, their experience of love is "a mere repetition" of one of those "moments of intense feeling" that are devoted to praise and appreciation. For this reason, they are caught up in the same dialectic that governs experience in general. As time passes, they must learn that physical passion is merely an expression or form of love, so that "as passion is less and less useful, love shines more and more out" (*EK*, 183). Then they must learn that even they themselves as individuals are merely symbols to each other of a mystery that includes them but also goes beyond them. As the drama unfolds, the lovers have the opportunity to become more and more conscious both of themselves and of their relation to the mystery:

Each becomes an unconscious symbol in the other's eyes, a symbol of love which is beautiful, but mistaking the symbol for the reality they overlook deformity and misery or else at last through ignorance become cynics. This is the commonest phenomenon of all. From the beginning of time, or of history at least, one has seen love, but trying to describe it, describes the symbol and in that love is so much greater than its terms finds it impossible not to magnify, impossible not to think that here, in the symbol, is the greatest beauty of all. But often this symbol is suddenly destroyed when we see at last that love is not anything mortal, that it flows over the forms of the world like water that comes and withdraws. Yet as the objects of life are all we can know love by, this coming and going discloses us to be involved in a destiny more than we can imagine, which must be very marvelous. (*EK*, 184)

"Love," then, being one of the primary names of the nameless truth, Williams concludes his essay by declaring that "it goes beyond life, where no knowledge goes and is the most daring of all the mysteries and the most wonderful, which is a sufficient pretext for the presence here of man" (*EK*, 185).

What then of service? "Service" is the term Williams uses to designate the highest expression of love of which man is capable, for it refers not to fidelity with respect to the beloved but rather to fidelity with respect to the mystery. The ordinary kinds of service that have a practical application in everyday life are to be admired, but more admirable still is the desire to communicate to

others our own sense of the ultimate reality. Thus "our only service" of any real consequence is "to give praise, to put into form
what we see" (*EK*, 185). In this way, not only what we see but,
more importantly, we ourselves in our own persons come to symbolize the mystery we praise. In bearing witness to the mystery, we
deliberately become its chief vehicle, its chief form of expression.
In fact, it is not so much that we express the mystery as it is that the
mystery expresses itself in us and through us. It is in this sense that
"service" may be defined as fidelity to the mystery: it is "to believe
proudly in love as a law and to stand for this clear intellectual be-
lief permanently, so that a form be given to the reality in your own
person, than which there is no greater praise, which it solely is"
(*EK*, 185). If in the beginning there is only the "I" facing the Unknown, consumed by wonder to such a degree that everything else
becomes subordinate to our act of admiration, in the end there is
only the "I" representing the Unknown, the "I" as the ultimate
image of the imageless truth. The whole world and everything it
contains offers itself as material for effecting or demonstrating this
higher revelation.

The argument of "Love and Service," while not explicitly idealistic in a philosophical sense, is nevertheless compatible with the
idealism of Williams' other writings, for it makes the drama of consciousness the thing of main importance. The absolute foundation
of all that concerns us is an act of mind, an act of apprehension,
wherein the phenomenal world is used as a means to an end. Indeed,
the phenomenal world from the very beginning is radically symbolic, referring simultaneously to the "I" and to the unknown mystery. The sun and the moon in Williams' analysis are never mere
objects in their own right. They are one thing to the native who
uses them as instruments of praise, something else to the scientist
who explains them, but always one thing or another according to
the nature of the mind that perceives them. The fall occurs when
the phenomenal world assumes (for the mind of a fool, as Blake
would say) the character of a thing in itself, a finality, a fixity, independent of the mind that perceives it. No longer functioning as
a symbol or as a set of symbols, it becomes that "solid apparition"

Williams decries so eloquently in the "Prologue" to *Kora in Hell*. It becomes the "natural or scientific array," "the walking devil of modern life" (*I*, 14). The fall, then, is really an abnegation of self, a denial of consciousness as the essential component of that which is experienced. Indeed, from Williams' point of view, the super-structures of science and philosophy represent a massive exercise in self-alienation wherein the mind constructs, in opposition to itself, an infinitely complex "reality" to which it then fancies itself inferior and subordinate. It is precisely to combat this illusion that Williams takes upon himself the task of being a poet. Against the "solid apparition" of an independent reality he sets himself—a free, autonomous spirit—the very picture of Emersonian self-reliance. By establishing his own freedom and his own autonomy with respect to the so-called real world (which he does by using whatever parts of that world he chooses in whatever way he pleases for the purposes of his art), he also establishes the autonomy and freedom of the formless truth with respect to its own manifestations. *His* freedom and independence, which are exercised by "forever changing the sign," become the superlative image of *its* freedom and independence, so that by making all things a vehicle for himself he becomes a vehicle for it.

It cannot be emphasized too strongly that whatever Williams says in "Love and Service" about the formless truth or the unknown applies equally to the self—not to the finite, empirical self but to the transcendental self, the ego. At the deepest level, this self and the unknown are identical, as Williams makes clearer in some of his later pronouncements. The mystery about which nothing can be said except that it "is not anything mortal" and that it "flows over the forms of the world like water that comes and withdraws," is not finally distinguishable from the "rare element" that Williams in his *Autobiography* claims to have been pursuing all his life, the "rare presence" that "will not use the same appearance for any new materialization" (*A*, 362). After thirty-five years, he still calls it "the thing I cannot quite name," "the thing . . . of which I am in chase" (*A*, 288). Its true location, despite the fact that its appearances are shifting and fleeting, is "in the self," in the "secret gardens of the self" (*A*, 288). It is "our very life," it is "we ourselves" (*A*, 362). "Within us," as Williams says in his "Advice to the Young Poet," "lies imprisoned the infinitely multiplex quarry . . . a nascent thing, a variety, living and firm."[3] That is why he can claim of the work of art that it "makes the unknown a form which eyes, ears, nose, mouth, and fingers can experience" while at the same time, and for that very reason, it allows man "to say, *I am*, in concrete terms" (*ARI*, 212). "I am" equals "the Unknown."

One of the most important consequences of the myth of the fall as it is presented in "Love and Service" is that it enables Williams to remain perpetually dissatisfied with all current expressions of the formless truth, including his own. On the one hand, he can look back with nostalgia to a hypothetical past when a relatively pure, unsophisticated consciousness prevailed and expression was "true." On the other hand, he can also look forward to an equally hypothetical future when the effects of our apostasy shall be completely reversed and "men shall come to the great altar of the Unknown with pomp and singing and processions" (*EK*, 181). Such a prospect gives him the opportunity to denigrate the present moment and to find the conditions of art and experience inadequate as they now exist. Indeed, the myth of the fall is more than just a pseudo-historical explanation of the loss and recovery of the autonomy of consciousness vis-à-vis the world. It is also an instrument of criticism, a pretext for passing negative judgments on contemporary culture—something Williams has to be able to do in order to avoid idolatry. He has to be in a position to reject every manifestation of the "rare presence" in order to affirm his own spiritual autonomy and to affirm the fact that "the infinitely multiplex quarry" transcends its own finite embodiments.

Most readers have supposed that Williams was a keen admirer of all things here and now and that, consequently, he must have looked approvingly on the contemporary American scene and on modern art in general. Nothing could be further from the truth. The evidence indicates that while Williams certainly countenanced every attempt to escape from the present by dashing headlong toward the beckoning future, he took a very dim view of his own immediate culture and regarded the modern period, especially with respect to art, as a sort of Dark Age with only occasional flashes of promise. In *Paterson*, he looks back to an earlier time when "the word" lived in the ancient divisions of the poetic line, hoping it will live there again in a new measure. In our own time, however, "poetry is in an age of darkness" (*EK*, 129). Indeed, if we look carefully at what Williams has to say about his contemporaries, we find the myth of the fall almost everywhere implicit in his judgments, even when they are seemingly most generous.

In praising Joyce's work, for example, which he was not always prone to do, Williams calls attention to the way Joyce appears to *restore* the original qualities of words in his work after *Ulysses:*

> Joyce maims words. Why? Because meanings have been dulled, then lost, then perverted by their connotations (which have grown over them) until their effect on the mind is no longer what it was when they were fresh, but grows rotten as *poi*—though we may get to like *poi*.
>
> Meanings are perverted by time and chance—but kept perverted by academic observance and intention. At worst they are inactive and get only the static value of anything, which retains its shape but is dead. All words, all sense of being gone out of them. Or trained into them by the dull of the deadly minded. Joyce is restoring them. (*SE*, 89–90)

Joyce's work, then, is fundamentally conservative since he makes it possible for words "to be understood again in an original, a fresh, delightful sense" (*SE*, 90). In doing so, he resembles the surrealists, who, as Williams remarks on another occasion, "have invented the living defense of literature" by similarly emphasizing "the elusive reality of words": "It appears to be to them to knock off every accretion from the stones of composition. To them it is a way to realize the classical excellence of language, so that it becomes writing again" (*SE*, 96–97).

Williams himself tries to do something similar in his essays on American history, which he describes at the beginning of his book *In the American Grain* as essays in restoration or reconstruction. The truth about America lies dormant, unavailable, in history's "original records." Only the most vigorous efforts of interpretation can ferret it out and state it again, so that it becomes fresh once more: "In letters, in journals, reports of happenings I have recognized new contours suggested by old words so that new names were constituted" (*IAG*, v). In surmounting the obstacles imposed by "borrowed titles" and "misappellations," Williams hopes to deliver the spirit from the letter, "the strange phosphorus of the life" from the fossil records, by going back to a truth that precedes even the original documents, a truth that must be regarded as the source of all his sources. Indeed, his own activity as a historian may be compared to the pioneering activities of the men and women he writes about, those who left the old world of Europe to make a new beginning in America. They too, like him, may be thought of as voyagers into the past, leaving behind them the "modern" culture of Europe and sailing to a primitive, almost mythic, land of origins. In a sense, the New World was really the old world restored, a kind of golden age all over again. More than a place, it was "a beloved condition . . . in which all lived together" (*IAG*, 138), "in its every expression, the land of heart's desire" (*IAG*, 139). Always it seems, with the passage of time, this condition is lost, and so we must be continually returning to it: "However hopeless it may seem, we have no other choice: we must go back to the beginning; it must all be done over" (*IAG*, 215). That is what the Europeans were doing, and that is what we must do ourselves if we want to recover the original potential of the New World condition.

In the American Grain is, finally, a work of prophecy in which Williams urges us to repent by recalling us to the promise of the past. The question he poses again and again in these essays is this: to what extent does America today reflect the "beloved condition" of America as it used to be? The answer is that it reflects it hardly at all. Just as the "true character" of American history has been lost in a "chaos of borrowed titles," so the very essence of the New World spirit has been lost in the growth of American culture. America today is simply a wasteland of decay and ignorance. (Williams was writing this, it will be remembered, during the effervescent, sophisticated twenties.)

We believe that life in America is compact of violence and the shock of immediacy. This is not so. Were it so, there would be a corresponding beauty of the spirit—to bear it witness; a great flowering, simple and ungovernable as the configuration of a rose—that should stand with the gifts of the spirit of other times and other nations as a standard to humanity. There is none. (*IAG*, 174)

As Williams analyzes it, the rot set in almost from the very beginning so that only a few heroes like Père Sebastian Rasles, Daniel Boone, or Edgar Allan Poe, appear to have recognized what the New World could mean. For the most part, a vast cultural inertia has manifested itself all along in terms of a collective failure of consciousness, in "the niggardliness of our history, our stupidity, sluggishness of spirit, the falseness of our historical notes, the complete missing of the point." "In the confusion," it seems, "almost nothing remains of the great American New World but a memory of the Indian" (*IAG*, 157). Such despair is not totally unmitigated. Williams' own heroic attempt to revive the past by writing a book about it is meant to suggest the possibility at least of a more general revival in American life. The odds, however, are mostly against it. If the availability (to Williams) of historical truth implies the potential availability of the New World spirit to all the rest of us, still Williams will not allow us to forget that the most serious misconceptions are likely to prevail, their effects being as real and as terrible as Cortez's destruction of Tenochtitlan. Like the Puritans before us who had "nothing of curiosity, no wonder, for the New World" (*IAG*, 112), we are so degraded by our ignorance that it is doubtful whether we can ever make anything of our neglected opportunities:

The primitive destiny of the land is obscure, but it has been obscured further by a field of unrelated culture stuccoed upon it that has made that destiny more difficult than ever to determine. To this latter nearly all the aesthetic adhesions of the present day occur. Through that stratum of obscurity the acute but frail genius of the place must penetrate. The seed is tough but the chances are entirely against a growth. It is possible for every vestige of virtue from the New World to be lost, like the wood pigeon. (*IAG*, 212)

Skeptical as he was about the quality of contemporary culture as a whole, Williams was even more skeptical about the quality of modern art, especially the art of poetry. It is true he endorsed the experiments of the avant-garde, but he did so primarily because he regarded such experiments as protests against the prevailing spirit

of the times. The arts, he believed, had fallen into a state of ill
health, and drastic remedies alone promised to revive them. Here
too it was a question of going back to the beginning, of dismissing
the traditions that constituted his immediate heritage and returning
to principles that lay far back in the past. In the preface to his
Selected Essays, he reconsidered his long career and reached the
conclusion that all along he had been trying to reestablish the
validity of "ancient rules":

> Meanwhile I went on writing my poems. I had better say, construct-
> ing my poems. For I soon discovered that there were certain rules, cer-
> tain new rules, that I became enmeshed in before I had gone far, which
> I had to master. These were ancient rules, profoundly true but long
> since all but forgotten. They were overgrown with weeds like ruined
> masonry. Present teaching had very little to do with them, but that
> they existed I had no doubts; it remained only for me to rediscover
> them. (*SE*, Preface, [ix–x])

Did he, in fact, rediscover them and apply them successfully in his
own poetry? Did his contemporaries rediscover them? It is tempting to think so and even more tempting to suppose that Williams
thought so. In reality, however, he was perpetually haunted by a
sense of failure, not only with respect to his own work but also
with respect to the whole modernist endeavor. Even at the end,
when for a time he thought he had found a philosopher's stone in
the variable foot, the cloud of skepticism did not lift. Even then,
it seemed to him that poets were still just on the verge of writing
really splendid poetry, just on the verge of pinpointing the new
measure that would magically restore our lives and usher in the
millennium.

In 1921, he announced his hopes for American art in an editorial
for his new magazine *Contact*:

> We want to give all our energy to the setting up of new vigors of artistic
> perception, invention and expression in the United States. Only by slow
> growth, consciously fostered to the point of enthusiasm, will American
> work of the quality of Marianne Moore's best poetry come to the fore
> of intelligent attention and the ignorance which has made America an
> artistic desert be somewhat dissipated. (*SE*, 29)

This editorial set the stage for a series of complaints that can be
found scattered throughout Williams' writing during the 1920s. In

The Great American Novel, he observes that we have "no art," "no words": "I touch the words and they baffle me. I turn them over in my mind and look at them but they mean little that is clean. They are plastered with muck out of the cities" (*I,* 175). In *Spring and All* he writes in the same vein, noting that "the greatest characteristic of the present age is that it is stale—stale as literature" (*I,* 134). Indeed, the situation is dire, since "the most of all writing has not even begun in the province from which alone it can draw sustenance" (*I,* 129). Six years after *Spring and All,* Williams saw no reason to change his opinion. He writes in 1929, "There is very little light in literature today."[4] Despite the fact that poetry is "just at the brink of its modern development,"[5] for the moment, at least, "language is in its January" (*SE,* 96), having been "enslaved, forced, raped, made a whore by the idea venders" (*SE,* 96).

If much of this sounds like a polemic aimed at modernism's reactionary enemies, there can be no mistake about Williams' intentions in an important letter written to Kay Boyle in 1932. Here his criticisms are aimed squarely at the modernists themselves. In passing, he mentions ten writers, without most of whom the modernist movement would be inconceivable—Walt Whitman, Robinson Jeffers, E. A. Robinson, Robert Frost, Yvor Winters, Wallace Stevens, Gertrude Stein, James Joyce, T. S. Eliot, and Ezra Pound. Incredibly, not one of these writers can be said to provide a good model of what the modern poet ought to be doing. Thus, Williams concludes, "there is no clear perception of poetic form operative today," nor can there be any "until the poem itself appears as the rule in fact" (*SL,* 133). Since "the present moment," as far as poetry is concerned, is merely "a formless interim," since the term "modern poem" is virtually an oxymoron, the most satisfactory way of referring to the modern period would be to call it "the premasterly period":

It is a period without mastery, that is all. It is a period in which the form has not yet been found. It is a formative time whose duty it is to bare the essentials, to shuck away the hulls, to lay open at least the problems with open eyes. (*SL,* 133)

Ironically, the writers who have done their best to shuck away the hulls, such as Joyce and Stein, are also the ones who have most in-

hibited the positive development of new form. Joyce and Stein
have been paramount, claims Williams, "in knocking the props
from under a new technique in the past ten years and enforcing it.
They have specifically gone out of their way to draw down the
attention on words, so that the line has become pulverous instead
of metallic—or at least ductile" (*SL*, 129). Whatever their virtues,
their influence has been pernicious:

Some of the young men seem to me to be too much influenced by the
disintegrationists, the users of words for their individual forms and
meanings. They are after meanings (Joyce) and their objectivity as
things (Stein). Well, as far as poetry is concerned, what of it? (*SL*, 131)

Although he looks forward to a definite departure from these influences in the direction of "a metrical coherence of some sort"
(*SL*, 129), Williams as yet cannot see how to proceed. All he
knows is that "the modern line must have an internal tension which
is now nowhere" (*SL*, 135). The only poet who even comes close
to what Williams is looking for is Pound, and his work too is
merely a preparation for good things to come:

So far I believe that Pound's line in his *Cantos*—there is something *like*
what we shall achieve. Pound in his mould, a medieval inspiration, pat-
terned on a substitution of medieval simulacra for a possible, not yet
extant modern and living material, has made a pre-composition for us.
Something which when later (perhaps) packed and realized in living,
breathing stuff will (in its changed form) be the thing. (*SL*, 135)

For his own part, Williams claims to have achieved very little—just
"a few patches of metrical coherence which I don't as yet see how
to use" (*SL*, 130). Such is the situation as of 1932: a few patches of
metrical coherence, in the *Cantos* possibly a pre-composition, but
nowhere as yet "the poem itself." At their best, the modernists are
to be regarded as indispensable prophets crying in the literary wil-
derness, preparing the way with their relentless experiments, "long
before the final summative artist arrives" (*SE*, 103).

   In the 1940s, Williams' quest for form became increasingly ur-
gent. Still in pursuit of what he liked to call "the new measure,"
he made it clear in his essay "An Approach to the Poem" that considerable effort lay ahead:

do not believe, I keep repeating, that the form of the age will spontaneously appear; that is, that the great age will just accidentally find the unique representation of itself. . . . Nothing could be more fatuous. It is the work, the exhausting work of the artist who . . . will MAKE the world today.[6]

To Parker Tyler he related the following anecdote, which reveals how seriously he took his own, personal efforts to discover the principles of the modern poem. The anecdote concerns an incident that had occurred after one of Williams' public readings:

Someone in the audience . . . asked me if I thought I had given any evidence of the "new way of measuring" in anything I had read that night or in anything that I myself had written at any time. It was a fair question but one I shall have to postpone answering indefinitely. I always think of Mendelejeff's table of atomic weights in this connection. Years before an element was discovered, the element helium, for instance, its presence had been predicted by a blank in the table of atomic weights.

It may be that I am no genius in the use of the new measure I find inevitable; it may be that as a poet I have not had the genius to do the things I set up as essential if our verse is to blossom. I know, however, the innovation I predict must come to be. Someone, some infant now, will have to find the way we miss. Meanwhile I shall go on talking.

For one thing: what I see, the necessity which presents itself to me has already motivated and colored my critical opinions. I see many past writers in an entirely new light when I set them against the scale by which I am coming more and more to measure. And for myself, if I can write three lines—the day before I die, three lines inspired by the true principle by which I work—everything else, good or bad, in my life will have been justified.

Next time I'm going to speak of my own work only. As far as I am able I'm going to tear it apart in the light of my newer concepts. Either what I have done in the past has helped to clarify that or it has not. If it has not then it must be rejected and the reason for rejecting it shown lucidly. (*SL*, 243)

In the austerity of his requirements, if nothing else, Williams sounds like a latter-day Matthew Arnold. In 1947, he observed to Kenneth Burke: "For myself I reject all poetry as at present written, including my own. I see tendencies, nodes of activity, here and there but no clear synthesis" (*SL*, 257).

In the early 1950s, the long-awaited breakthrough seemed at hand. The new measure appeared to beckon to Williams in one of his own poems, the second book of *Paterson*, which provided an example of the triadic line, and Williams at last thought he was on the right track. To Martha Baird, he described himself as a man "who has been searching for a solid footing": "But at last I am just beginning to know, to know firmly what the present day mind is seeking. I finally have caught a glimmer of the basic place which we, today, must occupy."[7] In the *Autobiography* as well, there is a feeling of relief that comes with the suspicion that Eliot's influence is finally on the wane: "Only now, as I predicted, have we begun to catch hold again and restarted to make the line over" (*A*, 174–75).

But, despite these glimmerings of hope, Williams went right on talking as though the new measure were still to come, as though even his own efforts to use it were but crude approximations. Almost a year after the publication of *The Desert Music and Other Poems*, he was still lamenting that "the measure by which the poem is to be recognized has at present been lost" (*SL*, 331). The verse he approved of was still a verse he could only "envisage" (*SL*, 332). In his statement on measure for Cid Corman, Williams refers to the poems included in *The Desert Music* as "a few experiments," not to be taken as final: "There will be other experiments but all will be directed toward the discovery of a new measure" (*SE*, 340). In the same breath he admits "there is no one among us who is consciously aware of what he is doing." In 1958, the new measure is "beyond our thoughts."[8] In 1961, it is "what we must get to in the modern world."[9] No wonder, then, when Williams was contemplating the end of his career, he seriously considered grouping all his poems together under a singularly appropriate title—not the *Complete Poems* or the *Collected Poems* but *The Complete Collected Exercises Toward a Possible Poem*.[10]

The reason Williams' critical judgments are generally so negative, despite his (usually temporary) enthusiasms for the particular achievements of particular artists, is that he needs to be able to say at any given moment that a work of art or even whole schools of art are unsatisfactory, inadequate. He needs to be able to say that they are merely "perishable signs," which point beyond themselves to the formless truth. In saying so, Williams himself comes forward in his own person as the true representative of that which is formless; for it is not the work that matters so much as the power that calls it into being. That Williams understood the higher necessity of not finding the form he claimed to be seeking seems clear enough from his letter to John Riordan of 13 October 1926. There he explains that it is precisely his desire to "encircle" everything that makes it impossible for him to work inside determinate patterns:

But my failure to work inside a pattern—a positive sin—is the cause of my virtues. I cannot work inside a pattern because I can't find a pattern that will have me. My whole effort . . . is to find a pattern, large enough, modern enough, flexible enough to include my desires. And if I should find it I'd wither and die.[11]

Here Williams explicitly formulates the paradox of Hegel's romantic artist who seeks and uses determinate, sensuous forms but only in order to designate the freedom and indeterminacy (i.e., the absolute inwardness) of his own spiritual subjectivity. Perhaps a closer analogue to Williams' letter can be found in Emerson's "Circles," for Emerson was equally familiar with the romantic dilemma. In "Circles," he refers to himself as "an endless seeker," having learned that every pattern, or every circle, is less than the power from which it emanates:

Whilst the eternal generation of circles proceeds, the eternal generator abides. That central life is somewhat superior to creation, superior to knowledge and thought, and contains all its circles. Forever it labors to create a life and thought as large and excellent as itself, suggesting to our thought a certain development, as if that which is made, instructs how to make a better. (CW, II, 188)

Like Williams nearly a century later, Emerson was deeply concerned with the paradoxical relationship between self and world, between the formless truth and the perishable sign, which seems at once to require both the affirmation and the negation of the particular work of art. It is to Emerson, then, that we must apply ourselves if we would understand the American roots of Williams' American brand of idealism.

3 Emerson the Precursor

Imagination, indeed, is his single theme. As a preacher might under every text enforce the same lessons of the gospel, so Emerson traces in every sphere the same spiritual laws of experience—compensation, continuity, the self-expression of the Soul in the forms of Nature and of society, until she finally recognizes herself in her own work and sees its beneficence and beauty. His constant refrain is the omnipotence of imaginative thought; its power first to make the world, then to understand it, and finally to rise above it.

—SANTAYANA, *Interpretations of Poetry and Religion*

For Williams, the problem of the fall is identical with the problem of symbols, for if symbols are the means whereby the unknown first impinges on our awareness, they are also the means whereby we lose our awareness and fall into idolatry. If, therefore, our original apprehension of truth takes the form of an affirmation of the symbol, our ultimate apprehension of it must take the form of a negation of the symbol which is accomplished by "forever changing the sign." In America no one has wrestled with this problem more conspicuously than Emerson, which probably explains why Emerson, more than any other writer, provides a key to Williams. The two reached the same conclusions because they shared the same motivations: a deep reverence for particular forms and an even deeper abhorrence of idolatry.

At least four years before the publication of his first book, *Nature*, Emerson stated his fundamental principles with great clarity in his farewell sermon on the institution of the Lord's Supper. He explains in this sermon that the institution is outdated, having ceased to communicate the spiritual nourishment with which it was originally associated:

> Passing other objections, I come to this, that the use of the elements, however suitable to the people and the modes of thought in the East, where it originated, is foreign and unsuited to affect us. Whatever long usage and strong association may have done in some individuals to deaden this repulsion, I apprehend that their use is rather tolerated than loved by any of us. We are not accustomed to express our thoughts or emotions by symbolical actions. Most men find the bread and wine no aid to devotion, and to some it is a painful impediment. To eat bread is one thing; to love the precepts of Christ and resolve to obey them is quite another. (*CE*, XI, 18–19)

Making every effort to separate the spirit of Christ's teaching from the forms and ordinances of institutionalized ritual, Emerson claims to be carrying out the principles of the first Christians:

> That for which Paul lived and died so gloriously; that for which Jesus gave himself to be crucified; the end that animated the thousand martyrs and heroes who have followed his steps, was to redeem us from a formal religion, and teach us to seek our well-being in the formation of the soul. The whole world was full of idols and ordinances. The Jewish was

a religion of forms; it was all body, it had no life, and the Almighty God was pleased to qualify and send forth a man to teach men that they must serve him with the heart; that only that life was religious which was thoroughly good; that sacrifice was smoke, and forms were shadows. This man lived and died true to this purpose; and now, with his blessed word and life before us, Christians must contend that it is a matter of vital importance,—really a duty, to commemorate him by a certain form, whether that form be agreeable to their understandings or not. Is not this to make vain the gift of God? Is not this to turn back the hand on the dial? Is not this to make men,—to make ourselves,—forget that not forms, but duties; not names, but righteousness and love are enjoined; and that in the eye of God there is no other measure of the value of any one form than the measure of its use? (*CE*, XI, 22–23)

Clearly, in all of this Emerson does not deny the importance or value of forms as such. At one point in the sermon he even says that "forms are as essential as bodies." But "to exalt particular forms," he insists, "to adhere to one form a moment after it is outgrown, is unreasonable, and . . . alien to the spirit of Christ" (*CE*, XI, 20). Obviously, in Emerson's attitude toward "particular forms" one may see the prototype of Williams' attitude toward "perishable signs," as evidenced in "Love and Service."[1]

Emerson, of course, grew less certain as time went on that even Christ's precepts were deserving of total commitment. In the process of clarifying and extending the principles announced in his sermon, he came to regard even these as mere manifestations, mere forms—like the bread and wine of communion. Throughout his voluminous writings, he keeps making the same point over and over again. Every philosophy and every religion, all doctrines and all rituals, are to be revered to the extent that they necessarily express the moral sentiment, which resides within us but which also responds to, and participates in, what is commonly termed God. However, each and all are to be rejected as soon as they displace that sentiment and become objects of devotion or of interest in their own right. Since Christianity has developed into what Emerson regards as the idolatrous worship of Jesus, Christianity too has become a form that has outlived its usefulness. It is the spirit, not the letter, of Christ's teaching that Emerson would have us admire:

The idioms of his language, and the figures of his rhetoric, have usurped the place of his truth; and churches are not built on his principles, but on his tropes. Christianity became a Mythus, as the poetic teaching of Greece and of Egypt, before. (*CW*, I, 81)

In "The American Scholar," Emerson complains, as he does in the "Divinity School Address," that "the sacredness which attaches to the act of creation,—the act of thought,—is instantly transferred to the record":

The soul active sees absolute truth; and utters truth, or creates. In this action, it is genius. . . . The book, the college, the school of art, the institution of any kind, stop with some past utterance of genius. This is good, say they,—let us hold by this. They pin me down. (*CW*, I, 56–57)

For Emerson, as for Williams, this is the true fall of man. At all times and in all places, the original perceptions of genius, the spontaneous expressions of "the soul active," are transmogrified into rigid systems, thereby becoming the focus of an idolatrous worship. Just as Williams wants to distinguish between the act of praise and the symbols used to embody the act, so Emerson is deeply suspicious of every attempt to equate the power within us and the symbolic expressions wherein that power manifests itself. He too considers this power to be an unknown mystery about which nothing can be said. In the "Divinity School Address," he speaks of "certain divine laws" which, though "we read them hourly in each other's faces, in each other's actions, in our own remorse," nevertheless "refuse to be adequately stated": "They will not . . . be written out on paper, or spoken by the tongue. They elude, evade our persevering thought" (*CW*, I, 77). In "The Over-Soul," he makes it clear that we ourselves, in our own persons, are merely manifestations or expressions of a power working in us and through us:

From within or from behind, a light shines through us upon things, and makes us aware that we are nothing, but the light is all. A man is the facade of a temple wherein all wisdom and all good abide. What we commonly call man, the eating, drinking, planting, counting man, does not, as we know him, represent himself, but misrepresents himself. Him we do not respect, but the soul, whose organ he is, would he let it appear through his action, would make our knees bend. When it breathes through his intellect, it is genius; when it breathes through his will, it is virtue; when it flows through his affection, it is love. (*CW*, II, 161)

In its "pure nature," however, the soul is indescribable. Though "we know that it pervades and contains us," it remains "undefinable, unmeasurable." Similarly, in "Experience," Emerson dismisses all the traditional names of what he refers to as "the Power which abides in no man and in no woman, but for a moment speaks from this one, and for another moment from that one" (*CE*, III, 58):

> Fortune, Minerva, Muse, Holy Ghost,—these are quaint names, too narrow to cover this unbounded substance. The baffled intellect must still kneel before this cause, which refuses to be named,—ineffable cause, which every fine genius has essayed to represent by some emphatic symbol, as, Thales by water, Anaximenes by air, Anaxagoras by (Νουσ) thought, Zoroaster by fire, Jesus and the moderns by love; and the metaphor of each has become a national religion. (*CE*, III, 72–73)

Above all things, Emerson wished to ride the crest of this ineffable power, and he was willing to sacrifice every limited conception of it in order to do so. Perpetual iconoclasm, for him as for Williams, is the one technique for remaining perpetually faithful—not to perishable signs but to the reality behind such signs. In "Circles," therefore, Emerson cheerfully repudiates even his own "once hoarded knowledge" as "vacant and vain," since the only thing that really matters is to participate as directly as possible in that "central life" which is "superior to creation, superior to knowledge and thought," and which labors forever "to create a life and thought as large and excellent as itself" (*CW*, II, 188). In the last analysis, all things which are not the ultimate mystery must drop away for both Emerson and Williams, making it clear that (in Emerson's phrase) "the soul gives itself alone, original, and pure, to the Lonely, Original and Pure, who, on that condition, gladly inhabits, leads, and speaks through it" (*CW*, II, 174–75).[2]

How does the soul accomplish this gift of itself? By refusing to traffic at all with symbols? By withdrawing into itself in utter disregard of the phenomenal world? On the contrary, the soul saves itself from being imposed upon by particular symbols by making all things equally symbolic, by using or interpreting all things as symbols of itself. It escapes the tyranny of things by rigging itself into power over things. That is the essence of Emerson's first major proclamation in *Nature*. He tells us to close our secondary texts— our textbooks of science, philosophy, and theology—and to go directly to Nature, not because Nature is not a text but because it is a text that we as individuals write for ourselves. By going back to Nature—as it were, back to our own primary experiences—we recover authority over the world and cancel our subjection to "authorities," whether they be great men or great books or powerful institutions. We awaken, as though by a miracle, from the long sleep of dogmatism and become conscious, perhaps for the first time, of our own centrality. We see all at once that Nature is not a thing in itself but "a metaphor of the human mind" (*CW*, I, 21). This brings us around full circle with respect to the problem of expression, for it gives us the right to regard the natural world as a sort of original language wherein the self or soul is already expressed apart from and prior to the fixities and distortions of institutionalized knowledge. Since "every word which is used to express a moral or intellectual fact, if traced to its root, is found to be borrowed from some material appearance," it follows, for Emerson, that the appointed function of "the outer creation" is "to give us language for the beings and changes of the inward creation" (*CW*, I, 18). Furthermore, since "every appearance in nature corresponds to some state of the mind," it would seem that "that state of the mind can only be described by presenting that natural appearance as its picture" (*CW*, I, 18). This idea is, of course, Emerson's contribution to the concept of the objective correlative, the concept that lies at the heart of Williams' interpretation of imagism.

The consequences of Emerson's theory of nature as language are far-reaching with respect to his conceptions of art and poetry, for what chiefly distinguishes the artist or the poet from other men in Emerson's eyes is the awesome power he alone possesses to make nature say his thoughts. While the philosopher or the theologian or the scientist labors to think in terms of a language abstracted from the original language of nature, and while the ordinary man simply follows along in the barren tracks of his superiors with little or no awareness that he is doing so, the poet in particular makes a conscious, heroic effort to "pierce this rotten diction and fasten words again to visible things" (*CW*, I, 20). More than any other language, then, the poet's language, when it is ideally successful, reflects that "original relation to the universe" (*CW*, I, 7) that both Emerson and Williams regard as our birthright and goal, temporarily misprized owing to the effects of a false, sophisticated culture. That is why Emerson calls the poet, in "Poetry and Imagination," "a true re-commencer, or Adam in the garden again" (*CE*, VIII, 31). Indeed, Emerson's poet is remarkably akin to Williams' native in that both use natural facts as expressive symbols—Emerson explicitly comparing the figurative expressions of poetry to the concrete speech of children and savages (*CW*, I, 18). He is even more akin, however, to Williams' conscious artist because, like Williams' artist, he knows he is using symbols, and consequently, to that extent he too is separated from the naïvety that characterizes original consciousness. His is not the consciousness that falls into idolatry but rather the consciousness that preserves itself from idolatry to the degree it recognizes "the independence of the thought on the symbol, the stability of the thought, the accidency and fugacity of the symbol" (*CE*, III, 20). As proof of his recognition of this fact, the truly regenerate poet according to Emerson, continually demonstrates his power "to make free with the most imposing forms and phenomena of the world, and to assert the predominance of the soul" (*CW*, I, 33):

He unfixes the land and the sea, makes them revolve around the axis of his primary thought, and disposes them anew. Possessed himself by a heroic passion, he uses matter as symbols of it. The sensual man conforms thoughts to things; the poet conforms things to his thoughts. The one esteems nature as rooted and fast; the other, as fluid, and impresses his being thereon. To him, the refractory world is ductile and flexible; he invests dust and stones with humanity, and makes them the words of the Reason. The imagination may be defined to be, the use which the Reason makes of the material world. (*CW*, I, 31)

Since every natural fact is informed by the human spirit that

consciously or unconsciously gives it its meaning, every natural
fact is, in its own way, a microcosm of the spirit wherein we find,
most unexpectedly, the very thing that has seemed to elude us:
"Thus is the unspeakable but intelligible and practicable meaning
of the world conveyed to man . . . in every object of sense"
(*CW*, I, 29). The mystery about which nothing can be *said* is
everywhere *shown* to us in the details of the phenomenal world.
This opens up the most remarkable possibilities for poetic expression just when it appeared that expression was impossible, because
it means that each of these details can in itself be regarded as a
poem. Any object, any thing, any person, indeed any group of
words, can be interpreted as a full revelation of the power that refuses to be named. And so we come to the other side of the tran-
scendentalist coin, the side that permits Emerson to display his
affection for particular forms. As he writes in "The Poet":

> There is no fact in nature which does not carry the whole sense of na-
> ture; and the distinctions which we make in events and in affairs, of low
> and high, honest and base, disappear when nature is used as a symbol.
> Thought makes everything fit for use. . . . Small and mean things
> serve as well as great symbols. The meaner the type by which a law is
> expressed, the more pungent it is, and the more lasting in the memories
> of men; just as we choose the smallest box or case in which any needful
> utensil can be carried. Bare lists of words are found suggestive to an
> imaginative and excited mind; as it is related of Lord Chatham that he
> was accustomed to read in Bailey's Dictionary when he was preparing
> to speak in Parliament. The poorest experience is rich enough for all
> the purposes of expressing thought. Why covet a knowledge of new
> facts? Day and night, house and garden, a few books, a few actions,
> serve us as well as would all trades and all spectacles. We are far from
> having exhausted the significance of the few symbols we use. We can
> come to use them yet with a terrible simplicity. It does not need that a
> poem should be long. Every word was once a poem. (*CE*, III, 17–18)

Here, with prophetic fervor, Emerson anticipates both the truncated means and the truncated subject matter of a good deal of
modern poetry. Here, concisely, are the principles of an aesthetic
which, as Thomas R. Whitaker points out, results eventually in the
"terrible simplicity" of "The Red Wheelbarrow" or "The Locust
Tree in Flower."[3] Seeing the whole in the part, the extraordinary

in the commonplace, the universal in the particular, or the super-
natural in the natural, means focusing ever more sharply and narrowly on minutiae. It means noticing things like "the meal in the
firkin; the milk in the pan; the ballad in the street; the news of the
boat; the glance of the eye; the form and the gait of the body"
(*CW*, I, 67)—just the sort of things that appear routinely in Williams' poetry. But it can also mean depending on verbal minutiae
to render these things, on bare lists of words cut loose from conventional syntax. It means or may come to mean the blowing up of
conventional poems, those "gaudy" fables Emerson speaks of in
Nature, and the rescuing of shards and fragments to put in their
stead—the substitution, finally, of verbal actions and relations for
the loftier actions and relations of human characters. Indeed, what
is partly anticipated here is the modernist shift from subject to
technique, from the poem as statement of fact or commentary on
reality to the poem as nonparaphrasable verbal artifact. When Williams remarks that "there are no sagas" anymore—"only trees now,
animals, engines" (*SE*, 68), or when he declares himself willing to
accept as poetry even "an arbitrary confusion of consonants and
vowels"[4] if it be truly novel, or a fashionable grocery list, if it
form "a jagged pattern" that can be identified as "a sample of the
American idiom" (*P*, 262), he is clearly following in the track of
Emerson.

Since, as Emerson believes, "all the laws of nature may be read
in the smallest fact" (*CW*, II, 201), or, as Williams says, the whole
world may be "contracted to a recognizable image" (*PB*, 42) or
"narrowed to a point" (*CLP*, 20), one of the artist's primary duties
must be to isolate and define particular objects, or aspects of objects, for purposes of reflection. Emerson touches on this idea in
Nature when he says that "the poet, the painter, the sculptor, the
musician, the architect, seek each to concentrate this radiance of
the world on one point" (*CW*, I, 17). He goes into the matter in
more detail, however, in the essay on art that concludes his first
series of essays, again anticipating the reductionist aesthetics of
Williams. There he observes that the power of art is the power "to
fix the momentary eminency of an object":

We are immersed in beauty, but our eyes have no clear vision. It needs, by the exhibition of single traits, to assist and lead the dormant taste. . . . The virtue of art lies in detachment, in sequestering one object from the embarrassing variety. Until one thing comes out from the connection of things, there can be enjoyment, contemplation, but no thought. . . . Love and all the passions concentrate all existence around a single form. It is the habit of certain minds to give an all-excluding fulness to the object, the thought, the word, they alight upon, and to make that for the time the deputy of the world. These are the artists, the orators, the leaders of society. The power to detach, and to magnify by detaching, is the essence of rhetoric in the hands of the orator and the poet. (*CW*, II, 210–11)

As soon as one realizes that the object so sequestered may be a person as well as a thing, or the verbal structure of a poem considered without respect to meaning or reference, then it becomes clear that Emerson's conception of art provides a scaffolding not only for the techniques of imagism but also for those of objectivism.[5] Thus Williams compliments the painter Charles Sheeler for having an "eye for the thing" which enables him to perceive the uniqueness and the individuality of his materials:

To discover and separate these things from the amorphous, the conglomerate normality with which they are surrounded and of which before the act of "creation" each is a part, calls for an eye to draw out that detail which is in itself the thing, to clinch our insight, that is, our understanding, of it. (*SE*, 233)

Similarly, in a letter to Louis Zukofsky written in 1928, Williams praises Zukofsky for having written a poem whose effect is that of a "thing," adding significantly that "there are not so many things in the world as we commonly imagine" (*SL*, 94). For Williams too, the power of art is largely the power to concentrate all existence around a single form. "The poem alone focuses the world" (*SE*, 242), becoming in every instance a microcosm, "a complete little universe" (*P*, 261), and expressing simultaneously "the whole life of the poet" (*P*, 261).

Nevertheless, for all his emphasis on the eminency of the object, Emerson never permits us to forget that it is strictly temporary. Other objects and other events come to our attention and the restless spirit moves on to appropriate them.[6] Accordingly, every work of art, however excellent, must sooner or later look "cold and false before that new activity which needs to roll through all things, and is impatient of counterfeits, and things not alive" (*CW*, II, 216). And so Emerson rounds out his paradox by reaffirming the predominance of the soul, not only with respect to natural facts but also with respect to works of art. Since "the truth was in us, before it was reflected to us from natural objects" (*CW*, II, 201), it is the object's function to lead us back to a clearer recognition of the sublimity of the self. Apart from this function, the object has no intrinsic value whatsoever. Even those objects that are the products of the highest human art—the most wonderful paintings, poems, and sculptures by the world's greatest artists—are but "signs of power," "billows or ripples" of "the stream of tendency," "tokens" merely of the need to create:

Art should exhilarate, and throw down the walls of circumstance on every side, awakening in the beholder the same sense of universal relation and power which the work evinced in the artist, and its highest effect is to make new artists. (*CW*, II, 215–16)

Thus, while "there seems to be a necessity in spirit to manifest itself in material forms" (*CW*, I, 22), there is an equally imperious necessity in spirit to withdraw itself out of material forms in order to contemplate its own intrinsic essence. The spirit embodied in a work of art, in that it belongs equally to all, reconstitutes itself—comes back to itself—in the spirit of the man or woman who perceives the work for what it is—a sign of power. It is in this sense, then, that "the soul is superior to its knowledge; wiser than any of its works":

The great poet makes us feel our own wealth, and then we think less of his compositions. His best communication to our mind, is, to teach us to despise all he has done. Shakspeare carries us to such a lofty strain of intelligent activity, as to suggest a wealth which beggars his own; and we then feel that the splendid works which he has created, and which in other hours, we extol as a sort of self-existent poetry, take no stronger hold of real nature than the shadow of a passing traveler on the rock. The inspiration which uttered itself in Hamlet and Lear, could utter things as good from day to day, forever. Why then should

I make account of Hamlet and Lear, as if we had not the soul from which they fell as syllables from the tongue? (*CW*, II, 171)

As an idealist, Emerson cannot avoid the conclusion that it is the subject that constitutes the essence of the object, and so it is to the subject that we must return in the course of our meditations on the object:

The subject is the receiver of Godhead, and at every comparison must feel his being enhanced by that cryptic might. Though not in energy, yet by presence, this magazine of substance cannot be otherwise than felt; nor can any force of intellect attribute to the object the proper deity which sleeps or wakes forever in every subject. (*CE*, III, 77)

For Emerson, the work of art, like every other object, is a perishable sign, a sort of resting place or halfway house in the circuitous journey of the spirit. If it is not to become an idol or an end in itself, it must be interpreted finally as the merest trace of "an aboriginal Power" residing not only in the artist who produced it but also in the consciousness that perceives it. In the final analysis, the work derives its importance from the fact that it is an occasion, as well as an effect, of spiritual activity.

The really striking thing about Emerson's aesthetic theories is that they allow him to countenance an extraordinary interest in the details and aspects of the phenomenal world *within* the context of idealism. What seems at first the most outgoing, selfless affirmation of external existence as the true location of value or meaning turns out in fact to be the most thoroughly consistent egoism in which the soul makes everything into a vehicle for itself. That this is also the case with Williams will be shown presently; meanwhile, it is worth noting that the manifestation of subjectivity in terms of objective interests and representations is analyzed meticulously in Hegel's lectures on aesthetics, where it is already understood to be a characteristic of romantic art in general. As Hegel says:

In romantic art . . . where inwardness withdraws itself into itself, the entire material of the external world acquires freedom to go its own way and maintain itself according to its own special and particular character. Conversely, if subjective inwardness of heart becomes the essential feature to be represented, the question of which specific material of external actuality and the spiritual world is to be an embodiment of the heart is equally a matter of accident. For this reason the romantic inwardness can display itself in *all* circumstances, and move relentlessly from one thing to another in innumerable situations, states of affairs, relations, errors, and confusions, conflicts and satisfactions, for what is sought and is to count is only its own inner subjective formation, the spirit's expression and mode of receptivity, and not an objective and absolutely valid subject-matter. In the presentations of romantic art, therefore, everything has a place, every sphere of life, all phenomena, the greatest and the least, the supreme and the trivial, the moral, immoral, and evil; and, in particular, the more art becomes secular, the more it makes itself at home in the finite things of the world, is satisfied with them, and grants them complete validity, and the artist does well when he portrays them as they are.[7]

As Hegel sees it, "realistic" descriptions or mere presentations of external details do not interfere with the victory of inwardness over externality; they simply extend that victory in all directions. Moreover, although the artist may choose to express himself by means of such descriptions, that is to say, by presenting finite things as they appear, he is by no means compelled to do so. Other options exist, all of which make it possible for the poet to demonstrate his freedom—his power "to make free," as Emerson puts it—"with the most imposing forms and phenomena of the world" (*CW*, I, 33). Hegel makes this even clearer in another passage:

The aspect of external existence is consigned [in romantic art] to contingency and abandoned to the adventures devised by an imagination whose caprice can mirror what is present to it, *exactly as it is*, just as readily as it can jumble the shapes of the external world and distort them grotesquely. For this external medium has its essence and meaning no longer, as in classical art, in itself and its own sphere, but in the heart which finds its manifestation in itself instead of in the external world and *its* form of reality, and this reconciliation with itself it can preserve or regain in every chance, in every accident that takes independent shape, in all misfortune and grief, and indeed even in crime.[8]

Williams' emphasis on the power of the perceiver over each and every object of perception comports with the formulas of Hegel and Emerson almost perfectly, for according to Williams it is the perceiver's responsibility to assert himself vis-à-vis the object—by mastering it, by epitomizing it, by penetrating its secret, or even by choosing to ignore it. In one way or another, he must annihilate the object in its recalcitrant objectivity in order to use it as a means of self-expression. This is what the artist must do to the object on which he bases his work, and this is what the perceiver must do to the work itself when it comes to his attention. In "The American Spirit in Art," Williams developed a memorable analogy to explain this process, comparing the mind of the perceiver to an oyster and the object of perception to a grain of sand:

> Speaking to the high school pupils of my suburb I told them: Our heads are oysters. Take the oyster: A grain of sand enters its secret domain, in other words, between its shells. The poor oyster (living perhaps in Greenwich Village) unable, for cosmic reasons, such as not being able to spit it out, to get rid of its torment, frets over it, rolling it back and forth until, miracle of miracles, it makes of it a beautiful thing, a pearl! That is the artist at work. (*ARI*, 212)

Before entering the oyster's domain, the grain of sand is a thing-in-itself, a chimera, of no significance to the oyster whatsoever. Upon entering the oyster the grain becomes an irritant or a stimulant so that, by virtue of the oyster's own activity, the grain of sand is gradually transformed into a pearl. Williams, indeed, is careful to stress the fact that the beautiful result of this process comes "from the very essence of the oyster itself—it did not come from the remoteness of the seas but from that which to the oyster was indigenous, its own shell" (*ARI*, 214).

In using this analogy, Williams neatly reverses the implications given it by Henry Adams in *The Education of Henry Adams* where it is used as a metaphor of the vanity and blindness of human imagination closed in on itself and surrounded by the infinitely greater forces of the supersensual chaos. The difference between Williams and Adams is that, for Williams, authentic perception is always imaginative or creative. That is its strength, not, as Adams fears, its weakness. In *Kora in Hell*, Williams tells us that his mother has the power to see things with great "intensity of perception" precisely because she is "a creature of great imagination." Instead of allowing herself to be intimidated like Adams by vague apprehensions of what might exist outside of her own sphere, she focuses her attention on "the thing itself"—the grain of sand—and, by her own power, her own intensity, "she still breaks life between her fingers" (*I*, 8). Perception, then, is primarily an aggressive act, an act of mastery in which the perceiver concentrates his attention on a particular thing and, in doing so, detaches or separates it from "the world of make-believe, of evasion, in which we live" (*EK*, 114). What better way to nick the solidity of "the so-called natural or scientific array" and rescue a piece of it for our own purposes? Surely, this is what Williams has in mind when he talks about becoming coextensive with the universe. *My* world becomes *the* world. The world outside of me, the world according to the sciences, according to philosophy, according to the newspapers, even according to previous works of art, must be rejected as an illusion. In place of these false worlds, I must put the world according to me, the world as I happen to see it at any particular moment. Thus isolated and circumscribed by the mind of the perceiver, the thing perceived is acted on at will as an irritant or stimulant of the imagination's further labors. Only then, like the grain of sand, does it truly serve the purpose:

> The particular thing, whether it be four pinches of four divers white powders cleverly compounded to cure surely, safely, pleasantly a painful twitching of the eyelids or say a pencil sharpened at one end, dwarfs the imagination, makes logic a butterfly, offers a finality that sends us spinning through space, a fixity the mind could climb forever, a revolving mountain, a complexity with a surface of glass; the gist of poetry. *D.C. al fin.* (*I*, 81)

This paragraph from *Kora*, which explains how things challenge the mind by confronting it with what appear to be fixities or finalities, is followed immediately by a sentence that indicates the mind's overwhelming response. "There is no thing," says Williams, "that with a twist of the imagination cannot be something else." One hears in such a remark the authentic note of Emerson.

From his responses to specific works of art and his comments in general on the nature of art appreciation, it is certain that Williams adhered closely to the Emersonian concept of the work of art as a sign of power—a concept he would have to embrace given his own penchant for idealism. For Williams, the best works are unquestionably those that demand the most active imaginative response and those that bespeak the greatest mastery of materials. In confronting such works, he reasoned, we are given not only a vivid sense of the power of the artists who made them but also an unparalleled opportunity to exercise our own power as perceivers. In an unpublished manuscript entitled "What Is the Use of Poetry?" Williams suggests one of the ways we can use our power to break up the fixity or finality of a text. We can read it backwards, ignoring the established sequence of paragraphs:

This is a principle we can utilize to our profit in estimating the quality of any piece of writing: by reading it backward, paragraph by paragraph, from somewhere near the end back to the beginning and thus finishing. I find my own sensual pleasure greatly increased by so doing. I am much better able to judge of the force of the work in this way.[9]

There is a sense in which even a work of art confronts us with a finality that the senses "cling to in despair, not knowing which way to turn" (*I*, 14), so that we must "nick" it or tamper with it to prevent its becoming a solid apparition like the "natural or scientific array." Sometimes, however, the artist anticipates our need to tamper with his work by giving us fragments oddly arranged instead of a familiar sequence. In this way he prods us to respond more actively, more imaginatively, than we might do otherwise. By giving us fragments that are out of sequence or, at least, in an unfamiliar sequence, he invites us to rely on the authority and force of our own imaginations:

Some intimation of the character of this force may be discovered, I think, in the much greater interest felt in the snatches of pictures shown at the movies between the regular films, to advertise pictures coming the following week, than the regular features themselves. The experience is of something much more vivid and much more sensual than the entire film will be. It is because the banality of the sequence has been removed.[10]

Modernist works were especially interesting to Williams, because they seemed to require especially active responses. "Surely,"

he writes in an essay on Marianne Moore, "there is no poetry so active as that of today, so unbound, so dangerous to the mass of me-
diocrity, if one should understand it, so fleet, hard to capture, so
delightful to pursue" (*SE*, 123). The excellence in particular of
Miss Moore's poetry he attributes to the fact that "she despised
connectives." As a result, her poems become "exciting mazes" in
which the reader is encouraged to assume responsibility for "coming out at the right door in the end" (*SE*, 124). In the same fashion,
Williams attributes the excellence of *Ulysses* largely to the fact
that Joyce uses his power over language to force the reader "into
a new and special frame of mind favorable to the receipt of his
disclosure":

> By his manner of putting down the words it is discovered that he is
> following some unapparent sequence quite apart from the usual syn-
> tactical one. . . . He forces me, before I can follow him, to separate
> the words from the printed page, to take them up into a world where
> the imagination is at play and where the words are no more than titles
> under the illustrations. (*SE*, 28)

In his own poetry, Williams clearly tried to duplicate the qualities
he admired in the work of Marianne Moore and Joyce. In one of
his later essays, he tells us that over the years he learned to concentrate what he had to say "so that an alert mind is encouraged to take
the leaps necessary to bridge the gaps in the sense left to save time."
Such a mind willingly takes it upon itself "to reconstruct the sense
from the scheme, the grid of the words supplied."[11] Thus Williams explains his revision of "The Locust Tree in Flower" by
pointing out that the later version stimulates an increased effort on
the part of the reader:

> It was first written in full and published in my *Collected Earlier Poems*.
> Then I cut out everything except the essential words to leave the thing
> as simple as possible and to make the reader concentrate as much as
> he can.[12]

In all of this, it is evident that Williams no more regards the poem
on the page as "self-existent" than Emerson does. The grid of
words supplied on the page is merely a cue to the alert reader for
whom the real poem is an event, or series of events, that occurs in
his own mind.[13]

In 1932, in a letter to Ezra Pound, Williams tried to justify the obscurity of modern verse along these same lines. He tells Pound:

I've been playing with a theory that the inexplicitness of modern verse as compared with, let us say, the *Iliad*, and our increasingly difficult music in the verse as compared with the more or less downrightness of their line forms—have been the result of a clearly understandable revolution in poetic attitude. Whereas formerly the music which accompanied the words amplified, certified and released them, today the words we write, failing a patent music, have become the music itself, and the understanding of the individual (presumed) is now that which used to be the words. (*SL*, 125–26)

That is to say, the words have become a sort of running accompaniment to what goes on in the mind of the reader (or, for that matter, the mind of the poet). Their purpose or function is to amplify, certify, and release the ineffable process of thought. By shifting its locus from the page to the mind, the modern poem, says Williams, "puts it up to the reader to be a man—if possible" (*SL*, 126). Later, in an introduction to a volume of poems by Charles Henri Ford, Williams uses this theory to explain what he calls the "gist" of Ford's poems. That gist is "a special condition of the mind" that the poems generate. In themselves, so to speak, the poems constitute "a single continuous, running accompaniment (*SE*, 235) to this condition.

The power of the perceiver is virtually unlimited, according to Williams. Poems that invite us to use our power, poems that challenge us in a special way, may indeed be admirable, but in the last analysis our response to them always remains perfectly free, without constraint. If we so choose, we may even, without compunction, reject a poem. Such freedom to interpret, or not to interpret, can be seen in Williams' inconsistent responses to E.E. Cummings. Generally, Williams liked Cummings' work. One of Williams' essays even begins with the observation "e.e. cummings means my language" (*SE*, 263). In an article that appeared in *Arts Digest* in 1954, Williams makes a special point of saying that Cummings is not difficult to understand when his poems are approached in the proper spirit; and, in the course of demonstrating how to approach one of them, Williams remarks, "if you can understand one poem you can understand all" (*ARI*, 236). The point is not to worry about what Cummings says but rather to enjoy what he does with language. To enjoy the poem is to play with the poem in the same free spirit in which Cummings composed it:

> It is thrilling thus to have the lines reft of sense and returned to music.
> It is marvelous to be so intoxicatedly loosed along the page. We (as all poets feel) are free to cut diagonally across the page as if it were a field of daisies to lie down among them when the sun is shining "to loaf at our ease." (*ARI*, 236)

However, in spite of his own advice, Williams was considerably less enthusiastic three years later when he was interviewed by Mike Wallace.[14] Challenged by Wallace, who was clearly baiting him, Williams replied in the negative when asked if a passage of verse by Cummings ought to be regarded as poetry. "I would reject it as a poem," says Williams. "It may be, to him, a poem. But I would reject it. I can't understand it" (*P*, 261). The relative ease with which he delivers this judgment, his total lack of embarrassment despite the pressure of the situation, shows how completely he arrogated authority with respect to the object of his attention.

In fact, Williams was disgusted by the servility of what usually passes for art appreciation because such servility robs us of our own power. He liked Kenneth Burke's article on Laforgue, which appeared in *Contact* in 1921, because Burke was able to naturalize and acclimate and choose Laforgue for his own (to paraphrase "The Yellow Flower," *PB*, 91), thus dispelling the Frenchman's recalcitrant foreignness:

Laforgue in America is not the same man he is in France. Our appreciation recreates him for our special world if it is genuine. . . . Burke has taken what he wanted from the master in order to satisfy his own needs and his needs are the product of his world. (*SE*, 37)

Ultimately, the proper refusal to relinquish one's own authority necessitates the rejection of influences as well as the rejection of particular works:

> Any who would know and profit by his knowledge of the great must lead a life of violent opposites. The deeper at moments of penetration is his mastery of their work, the more vigorously at other moments must he fling himself off from them to remain a man himself. But if he

himself would do great works also only by this violence, this completeness of his wrenching free will he be able to use that of which their
greatness has consisted. (*ARI*, 119)

For Williams, then, the work of art is the result of an autonomous act of mind, and it makes possible, on the part of the perceiver, a similar act of mind. As with Valéry, so with Williams,
the fascinating thing about art is the creative (or recreative) process itself. It is the drama of the mind's activity that attracts Williams, in relation to which the sensuous result is to be regarded
mainly as evidence. We can observe this preoccupation again and
again in his essays as we watch him trying to get around a work,
trying to penetrate its secret in order to catch a glimpse of the mind
that produced it. Hardly ever does he admire a work without inquiring into this aspect of its significance.

A case in point is the essay "Cache Cache" on the surrealist
painter Pavel Tchelitchew. Williams' title refers, of course, to
Tchelitchew's painting *Hide-and-Seek*, the early sketches for
which Williams was permitted to see during a visit to Tchelitchew's studio. But the title of the essay also refers to the process
whereby all painters hide within their paintings the secrets of their
inner lives—disguising them but simultaneously revealing them
obliquely to the viewer who seeks them. Every artist, says Williams, not just the surrealist, needs to disclose and at the same time
conceal the "secret core" of himself; likewise every viewer who is
at all sensitive wishes to know what that secret core is. (An analogous situation with respect to poets is described in Williams' *Autobiography* where poems are defined as capsules "where we wrap
up our punishable secrets" [*A*, 343].) The adventure of looking
at a painting is therefore bound up in the struggle to "hit to the
base of the underlying purity from which ALL a man's work
emerges" (*ARI*, 124). The fact that Williams was not permitted to
see *Hide-and-Seek* as a finished painting but only as a series of preliminary sketches in no way diminishes the excitement of his struggle to grasp Tchelitchew's secret core. On the contrary, his excitement is increased because he is able to get that much closer
to the process that accounts for the painting. By looking at the

sketches and discussing them with the artist who made them, Williams is afforded the rare opportunity of watching the oyster at work transforming his grain of sand into a pearl. In describing this process of transformation, Williams takes for his metaphor the tree that constitutes Tchelitchew's ostensible subject. Thus he describes the drama of the painting's development:

A seed is planted. Well, there it lies, in the ground. The ground is a man's life partaking of life as a whole. Tchelitchew saw a tree and made a sketch of it in England ten years ago. There it lies. Very childish, very naïve. He says so himself. But it is a seed. Maybe it will grow, maybe it will die. In this case it grows. Five years later there is another sketch that has developed from the first. The seed did not rot. The tree is growing into a new area of the imagination. It was an old, gnarled tree to begin with. Now it is indulging in vagaries, it is getting new attributes that no other tree ever experienced. Children's faces, nine of them, are beginning to appear as outlines in the crotches between the trunk and the main branches. They have open mouths. The leaves, from the first red hands opening, through the extended full of the green maturity, to the mottled reds of winter approaching, assume their parts. (*ARI*, 125)

Here, it seems, Williams is concerned less with the interpretive process whereby the viewer detects faces in the tree than with the artistic process whereby Tchelitchew arrived at his conception of the finished painting. Having seen only the sketches, Williams understands this latter process better than if he had seen only the final product:

He showed us only the sketches he had made over several years, sketches slowly evolving into the thing; the organization, the composition on a flat surface, the seed that has developed, the shocking discovery it holds, the fulfillment it signalizes, the confession, the sweeping out, the purification of memory it represents, the nostalgia, the skills, the contempt, the humor, the despair, the translucence—summarizing poetry, flattening out superficial differences and resemblances—overfelt details, details that catch the eye as the thorns on a blackberry bush catch the hand and the sleeve as we reach for the fruit. (*ARI*, 125–26)[15]

In conclusion, Williams calls the painting "a hidden treasure," not because Tchelitchew refused to show it to him or because it represents the secret core of Tchelitchew's life, albeit obliquely, but because, in its own way, the painting is a new seed with an unforeseeable destiny, a new seed planted in the soil of American consciousness. All who see it in the Museum of Modern Art in New York have the same opportunity Tchelitchew had when he first saw the tree in England. Like an Emersonian circle, the painting will have been in vain for the beholder if it does not suggest to his thought a certain development, instructing him how to make a better.

The idea of art as a contact of mind with mind, as a reaching out of mind to mind, is enacted as well as described in Williams' illuminating commentary on Nicolas Calas' commentary on Hieronymus Bosch's *The Garden of Delights* (itself a commentary, according to Calas, on the thoughts of St. Gregory and St. Augustine). Williams' essay is full of admiration for Calas' skill in illuminating "the mind" of Bosch as revealed in Bosch's painting. *The Garden of Delights*, as it turns out, is also a "hidden treasure." It is "a riddle to be solved, for those with insight into the teachings of the saints" (*ARI*, 188)—a riddle for those who are of the same mind. Calas "anatomizes and develops the meaning" of the painting by showing that, in all its details, it reflects Bosch's reading of St. Gregory and St. Augustine. The objects and creatures that appear in the painting are endowed with the same significance they had for these saints:

They arise from these texts to the last detail. So that Bosch, by poring over them, knowing them by heart as a beloved reference, could have and indeed did derive [from them] the images he turned into the interrelated creatures and objects of his composition. (*ARI*, 189)

As far as Williams is concerned, Calas' scholarship is especially illuminating because, by making Bosch's painting more accessible to interpretation, it ends by making Bosch himself more accessible. Bosch himself comes alive as the genius behind the work. In his other paintings as well, he shows himself, says Williams, "to be a thinker of great force, a great user of the portrait as the means to an end—symbols to bespeak his mind" (*ARI*, 190). Nor is it Bosch's mind only that intrigues Williams; he is also intrigued by Calas' mind, for Calas has been completely successful, it would seem, in mastering the painting. If Bosch gives new currency to the thoughts of Gregory and Augustine, Calas does the same for Bosch, and that makes his mind as interesting as Bosch's. Like a proper idealist, Calas installs himself in the object of his consideration (the mind of Bosch) and recognizes therein his own animating spirit:

Calas's presentation is the work of a mind that puts itself on a par with Bosch, as though he too were contemporary and his picture, which before he painted it had its "creation" already extant in his consciousness, were a contemporary phenomenon—as it cannot but be—something alive today. Such a view gives the text new authority. It is no longer an explanation in which the present day attempts to put itself into conditions of the past which it cannot know and so stultifies itself. It is rather an evocation in which the present mind brings the past up to today and makes it work before our eyes. It is an eye cast into Bosch's mind, true enough, but it is also our eyes and mind which we lend to the past that it may live again as we watch it performing, alive before us. Calas lends Bosch his faculties and bids him speak. (*ARI*, 192)

By enabling us to see in *The Garden of Delights* "the image of how a contemporary mind, with all its shiftings of the subconscious, in dreams, in the throes of composition, works" (*ARI*, 193), Calas' commentary becomes "a detection of the light, the laying bare of a living flame, never out," "an evocation of an inner (continuous) meaning" which is "the inner meaning of our lives" (*ARI*, 195). This evocation is the only thing that matters finally, and "it is worth all our pains, all our efforts to keep that flame alive, to rescue it from desuetude" (*ARI*, 195), as much by tracing the career of its embodiments as by direct embodiment itself.

More striking than Calas' confrontation with Bosch or Williams' confrontation with Calas is the confrontation described in Williams' essay "The Portrait: Emanuel Romano." Indeed, two portraits emerged from the meeting of Williams and Romano—Romano's painting of Williams and Williams' essay on Romano. As Williams analyzes it, each man during the encounter contemplates the other and uses the other for his own expressive purposes. Romano paints not Williams' portrait but his own portrait—a self-portrait—using the terms or the contours of Williams' face. Williams, on the other hand, writes yet another exposition of his own idealist aesthetics using Romano as his chief exemplum. Each attains a "momentary eminency" for the other. Each becomes for the other a temporary vehicle for expressing the self. Thus Williams does not hesitate to ascribe to Romano (rightly or wrongly) his own artistic aims and interests. Harking back to the terms of "Love and Service," he concludes that Romano is trying desperately and with only partial success, since "he has not yet half revealed what he wants to say" (*ARI*, 205), to exhibit "the praise that is in him" (*ARI*, 204). There is a world in his head, says Williams, a world "different from the world we see . . . hidden from our eyes but in which he lives and moves and breathes":

> It is his business to show it to us, to convince our minds of its presence by painting it, placing it before us. It is the world of his imagination. It is the real world, the world that what *we* call real occludes. (*ARI*, 202–03)

To the extent Williams believes he can derive all of this from "the paintings themselves," he confirms to his own satisfaction that he too participates in the aboriginal power they reflect. Since both the essay he writes and the portrait Romano paints are evocations equally of the power "which sleeps or wakes forever in every subject" (to use Emerson's terms), both may be said to represent "a blossoming of the spirit" (*ARI*, 204).

Further examples of Williams' Emersonian habits of interpretation might well be adduced, but the time has come to consider more closely the nature of his own poetry. While it is true that virtually all of his poems assert the predominance of the self-conscious artist over natural facts as well as over the artistic medium, nevertheless there is a kind of development in Williams' work as he moves from the tenets of imagism to those of objectivism and from thence to a pursuit of the new measure. This development may be seen as an effort on Williams' part to make his poetry increasingly more expressive of the mental or spiritual power which is its true subject.

4 Poetry as Power

Our respect is not for the subject-matter, but for the creative power of the artist; for that which he is capable of adding to his subject from himself; or, in fact, his capability to
dispense with external subjects altogether, to create from
himself or from elements.

—POUND, *Gaudier-Brzeska: A Memoir*

WE are the center of the writing.

—WILLIAMS, *The Embodiment of Knowledge*

Though still regarded by many as an unintellectual poet, Williams was in fact a relentless theorist. In his *Autobiography*, he remembers the 1920s in particular as a time when "thinking, talking, writing constantly about the poem" was "a way of life" (*A*, 264), but the truth is there was never a time when he was not thinking, talking, and writing about the idea of poetry. The result of his speculations was that, over the years, he developed at least three different theories of the function of poetry. These theories are not unrelated to each other but they are difficult to reconcile with each other because each assumes that poetry has a different task to perform. The first theory, for example, assumes that the task of poetry is to report, with great accuracy and intensity, the poet's sensory experiences. When Williams tells us that it is the artist's duty to render exactly as it appears "what actually impinges on the senses . . . untouched" (*SE*, 119), or when he refers to such literary virtues as "simple clarity of apprehension" (*SE*, 71) or "integrity to actual experience" (*SE*, 118), he is speaking in terms of this first theory, which for convenience I shall call the imagist theory. According to this theory, the poem does well when it presents a faithful image of what the poet has seen or heard in his experience of the phenomenal world. The second theory assumes, conversely, that it is *not* the function of poetry to report experiences of things seen and heard but that a poem ought to *be* a thing in its own right—an objective, formal pattern devoid of representational or mimetic significance. When Williams defines the poem as "a small (or large) machine made of words" (*SE*, 256), he is speaking in terms of this second theory, which he calls objectivism. The third theory differs from both of the preceding theories in that it assumes that the function of poetry is primarily to exhibit, for purposes of contemplation, the speech rhythms detected in the spontaneous utterances of both the poet himself and his neighbors. In developing this third theory, Williams seeks to identify the essential spirit of the American idiom in order to liberate that spirit from the tyrannical impositions of conventional verse forms. Here the task of the poet is to isolate and employ in his poems a new measure capable of expressing without constraint the actual form of thought or feeling as it unfolds.

The imagist theory, the first of the theories to be developed, was in many respects superseded during the 1920s by Williams' preoccupation with objectivism. By the same token, objectivism appears to have been more or less superseded when Williams, at the latter end of his career, began to devote himself exclusively to the task of finding the new measure. At the same time, however, it must be said that Williams never really abandoned any of these theories, and, since he was in the habit of explaining himself in terms of whichever theory seemed most expedient at the moment, he has earned the reputation of being inconsistent and muddleheaded. This, I think, is unfair. Each theory is concerned with a different aspect of poetry, and, by refusing to consider the claims to importance of other aspects, each tries to defend in its own way the same basic principle—the principle of subjectivity. Furthermore, while it is true that Williams never relinquished the superficially incompatible goals of imagism and objectivism, there is a sense in which objectivism represents a logical progression from imagism, just as the quest for the new measure represents a similar development out of objectivism. By following this progression from the first theory to the second, and from the second to the third, we can begin to understand why the sort of poetry one finds in the *Collected Earlier Poems* gave way to the more meditative poetry of *Pictures from Brueghel*.

As Williams conceives it, the imagist poem is a poem that describes something—a person or an object, or a group of persons or objects gathered together in a single scene. Typically, with as little commentary as possible, the imagist poet tries to give us the thing itself, whatever it may be. He tries to make us see it and hear it just as he himself has seen it and heard it. At any rate, that is what he would like to do. In 1938, Williams stated the basic principle in simple terms: "In my own work," he explained, "it has always sufficed that the object of my attention be presented without further comment."[1] How can such a poem, devoted to the accurate description of objects, be interpreted as a defense of the poet's subjectivity? Why is it not, as it is usually supposed to be, a defense of the independence and objectivity of that which is described? The answer, of course, lies in Williams' idealism. From that standpoint, the imagist poem, based as it is on the personal observation of the poet, represents above all else the proper and legitimate return of authority to the observer. Confronted by the spectre of a "reality" rumored to be independent of him or indifferent to him—confronted, that is, by the spectral worlds of science, philosophy, art, and religion—the imagist poet sweeps all aside, affirming only that which he himself has experienced. In opposition to every account of *the world*, he sets his own world with himself as perpetual center. Thus, from Williams' point of view, the imagist poem is always implicitly an act of defiance against reality's official custodians—an act of rebellion, repeated again and again in accordance with the following prescription:

First rely on the direct observation of the senses, of such strength everything else is built up, without it nothing is reliable. Judge by the eyes and ears, touch and taste—reject everything from no matter what source that is without a place there. (*EK*, 135)

The difficulty involved in carrying-out this program is so enormous that every successful imagist poem must be regarded as an heroic triumph over tremendous odds. Not to see the poem against the background of the servility or apathy it opposes is to miss its significance entirely, for the imagist poem is a visible sign of the poet's having achieved success, at least for the moment, in his struggle to exercise authority over things. It is the climax of a drama which has to be inferred if the poem is to be appreciated properly but which is almost never made explicit in the poem itself, being excluded therefrom by the imagist aesthetic.

Without commenting on the drama, the imagist poem is submitted as tacit proof that the poet has somehow succeeded in rousing himself from what Williams calls "the plebeian plodding of ordinary consciousness" (*SE*, 306)—that he has somehow managed to avoid "the fragmentary stupidity of modern life, its lacunae of sense, loops, perversions of instinct, blankets, amputations, fullsomeness of instruction and multiplications of inanity" (*I*, 259). The proof lies in the fact that he has been able to discover and isolate "things" from "the amorphous, the conglomerate normality with which they are surrounded" (*SE*, 233). Thus the momentary eminency of "things" in the imagist poem has little or nothing to do with the intrinsic importance of the things themselves. Rather it signalizes a momentary intensification of the mental powers of the poet, so that the resulting poem may be construed as merely the conclusion or the end point of an action which cannot, by the very nature of the case, appear *within* the poem and of which the poet himself is the protagonist. In fact, the chief difference between Williams and his nineteenth-century predecessors seems to be that while they too are involved in the same heroic drama of consciousness, they tend to display the drama allegorically or in the process of meditation, whereas Williams tries to exclude it except by implication, having adopted, for the most part, the reductionist aesthetic advocated by Emerson and also, in a slightly different form, by Ezra Pound. Emerson and Pound both call for the use of extreme concentration based on the elimination of everything except "that detail which is in itself the thing" (*SE*, 233), and both assume that the presentation of such details is enough to communicate the inwardness of the poet. This, of course, is precisely what Pound means when he writes that "the natural object is always the *adequate* symbol."[2] If it is true that we find it difficult or impossible to say what we mean, it is also true, as much for Pound as for Emerson, that there is no need to *say* it; the thing itself, or rather the image of the thing, can *show* it by direct embodiment. Paradoxically, however, the poetry of direct embodiment is really the poetry of obliquity, since it uses the Emersonian technique of "terrible simplicity" not for the sake of the object but for the sake of personal expression.

In "Poetry and the Imagination," Emerson gives a sort of preview of the imagist argument in favor of combining extreme compression with the use of natural facts or natural objects to symbolize the self:

I require that the poem should impress me so that after I have shut the book it shall recall me to itself, or that passages should. And inestimable is the criticism of memory as a corrective to first impressions. We are dazzled at first by new words and brilliancy of color, which

occupy the fancy and deceive the judgment. But all this is easily for-
gotten. Later, the thought, the happy image which expressed it and
which was a true experience of the poet, recurs to mind, and sends me
back in search of the book. And I wish that the poet should foresee this
habit of readers, and omit all but the important passages. Shakspeare
is made up of important passages, like Damascus steel made up of old
nails. (*CE*, VIII, 32–33)

One is reminded here of Pound's later praise of Yeats for having
"boiled away all that is not poetic" in English poetry,[3] thus re-
ducing poetry to its own essence. For, indeed, the imagist poem is
precisely the important passage; the moment of clear apprehension
detached from the rest of consciousness; the thing itself cut away
from "the conglomerate normality"; the precipitate, finally, of a
process of exclusion or reduction—like the second version of Williams' "The Locust Tree in Flower," which offers an arrangement
of thirteen "essential words" from the original grouping of thirty-
four, or like Pound's "In a Station of the Metro," a thirty-line poem
pared down to two.[4] The irony, of course, is that while the imagist
poem has a climactic significance within the context of the poet's
experience, within the drama of consciousness, it cannot possibly
have such a significance for the uninitiated reader who encounters
it apart from its context. If the reader is unable or unwilling to reconstruct the context from the grid of the words supplied (or if he
refuses to invent a context—any context), he may well find the
poem flat and dull. The assumption that he will not find it flat and
dull depends on what amounts to an Emersonian faith in the objective correlative.

For Emerson and Pound, as well as for Williams, the expressive
power of the thing is explained by the fact that it is necessarily sat-
urated with the thought and emotion of the poet who uses it. Thus,
in Emerson's view, "A deep insight will always, like Nature, ultimate its thought in a thing. As soon as a man masters a principle
and sees his facts in relation to it, fields, waters, skies, offer to
clothe his thoughts in images" (*CE*, VIII, 17):

The mind, penetrated with its sentiment or its thought, projects it outward on whatever it beholds. The lover sees reminders of his mistress
in every beautiful object; the saint, an argument for devotion in every

natural process; and the facility with which Nature lends itself to the
thoughts of man, the aptness with which a river, a flower, a bird, fire,
day or night, can express his fortunes, is as if the world were only a disguised man, and, with a change of form, rendered to him all his experience. (*CE*, VIII, 11)

These two passages from "Poetry and the Imagination," together
with the following passage from "Intellect," constitute the very
core of the doctrine later preached by Pound and Williams as imagism. The poet, as Emerson writes in "Intellect," uses the image as
his "word":

If you gather apples in the sunshine, or make hay, or hoe corn, and
then retire within doors, and shut your eyes, and press them with your
hand, you shall still see apples hanging in the bright light, with boughs
and leaves thereto, or the tassled grass, or the corn-flags, and this for
five or six hours afterwards. There lie the impressions on the retentive
organ, though you knew it not. So lies the whole series of natural images
with which your life has made you acquainted, in your memory, though
you know it not, and a thrill of passion flashes light on their dark cham-
ber, and the active power seizes instantly the fit image, as the word of
its momentary thought. (*CW*, II, 198)

This, of course, is precisely Pound's explanation of his poem "In a
Station of the Metro." Intensely moved by the apparition of those
faces in the crowd, he sought at first to produce a verbal equivalent
of his emotion but without success. Indeed, "the first adequate
equation that came into consciousness" was a pattern of color, "little splotches of colour," so that, if Pound had been a painter, his
experience in Paris "should have gone into paint." Being a poet,
however, he sought and eventually found a verbal equivalent of his
emotion in the words "Petals on a wet, black bough." The image of
the petals on the bough is seized as the "word" that expresses
Pound's reaction to the faces. It is, as he says, "itself the speech.
The image is the word beyond formulated language."[5] For Pound,
then, it is not a question of the poet's expressing the world, it is a
question of the poet's expressing himself in terms of the world. The
image does not present things in the form of words so much as it
presents "an intellectual and emotional complex,"[6] otherwise unspeakable, in the form of things. By image, says Pound, "I mean
such an equation; not an equation of mathematics, not something

about *a*, *b*, and *c*, having to do with form, but about *sea*, *cliffs*, *night*, having something to do with mood."[7] Finally, as Pound explains in his "Affirmations—As for Imagisme," since it is the "emotional force" of the poet that "gives the image," "the 'organizing' or creative-inventive faculty is the thing that matters."[8] Pound's indifference to the task of making faithful artistic copies of external things, an indifference which enables him to embrace the increasingly abstract patterns of vorticism and which is explained by his primary interest in the inventive faculties of the poet, is as much an echo of Emerson's earlier attitude as it is an expression of the revolutionary aims of modernism. "The subject," writes Emerson, "is indifferent. Any word, every word in language, every circumstance, becomes poetic in the hands of a higher thought" (*CE*, VIII, 34). In fact, the essential mark of genuine poetry is that

it betrays in every word instant activity of mind, shown in new uses of every fact and image, in preternatural quickness or perception of relations. All its words are poems. It is a presence of mind that gives a miraculous command of all means of uttering the thought and feeling of the moment. (*CE*, VIII, 17)

Williams too insists again and again that the close description of objects and persons, such as one usually finds in imagist poetry, is not to be thought of as though it were undertaken for the sake of the persons and objects described. Rather, he suggests, such description is to be regarded primarily as a method of indirectly indicating the emotions of the person doing the describing. This point is made clearly enough in a book review, published in *The Little Review* in 1919, in which Williams takes Richard Aldington to task for having written some poems wherein, as Williams puts it, "one sees nothing." Instead of the vividly rendered scenes one would expect from a charter imagist like Aldington, Williams finds "an invitation to amnesia," an "amnesic invocation to love," which fogs over the values of the scenes and prevents them from being properly realized. A true imagist would know that the emotion of love is manifested in everything the lover sees. Thus a simple description of anything at hand would be sufficient: "A poet enkindled in his heart by love's desolateness or fruitfulness would see the light shine on the parapet at so acute an angle that the representation of it would—be a love poem."[9] Years later, when asked by James Laughlin to comment on some of Laughlin's own poems, Williams replied that the poems "would gain by having the thought made the spring-board for what the setup it indicates induces objectively in things": "If, in other words, you think this way, then it should induce you to see a hog or a wife or a fifty cent piece *that* way—whatever that way would be. That would be poetic creation."[10] On one occasion Williams went so far as to remind Pound himself that he was dangerously close to violating his own aesthetic principles in the *Cantos:* "You deal in political symbols instead of actual values, poetry. You talk about things (which you yourself have sufficiently damned in the past) instead of showing the things themselves in action" (*SL*, 249–50).

The most striking expression of Williams' faith in the objective correlative occurs, however, in the eighth section of his *Novelette* (1932), which is entitled "Anti-Allegory." There Williams tries to explain why conventional expressions of love are ineffective:

Love songs have always looked flat to me. Since what else is there to be written? But to attempt to state what is in effect the statement requires a subtlety that is rare—or an understanding which I have not yet found outside the difficulties which involve the expression I am detailing. . . .

Would you consider a train passing—or the city in the icy sky—a love song? What else? It must be so.

And if I told you the dark trees against the night sky and the row of the city's lights beyond and under them—would you consider that a love statement?

This is what my poems have been from the first. (*I*, 298–99)

Though Williams tends to scorn the use of figurative expressions, such as similes and metaphors, and though he loudly declares himself opposed to symbolism, he does so only because, like Emerson, he believes that the facts themselves are already perfectly symbolic, perfectly metaphorical. Without fail, they always, of necessity, designate his emotions:

Or a lit church. *There* is something you must understand, coming from me, in all frankness. What I would say has no relation to the effect of a church on the mind. It is so. It is, therefore, solely a song—when it is set down to be what is actually of no consequence in itself. . . .

As in this so every detail of the day—the lights of the city—in the distance that seem to close in together at the end of the dark street as the car swiftly advances: in themselves equal in detail the existence of affection—the fact of love and so, deciphered, intensely seen become in themselves praise and a song. (*I*, 299)

As Pound would say, the image is itself the speech; it is "the adequate symbol" for what the poet feels prompted to express. Poems like "Young Sycamore," "The Red Wheelbarrow," and "Between Walls" are explained by the fact that, in each case, Williams seizes the object of his immediate attention ("what is actually of no consequence in itself") and identifies it as the perfect receptacle of his innermost feeling. That is why every explanation of these and similar poems which stresses the intrinsic importance of the objects themselves misses the point.

Williams' own explanation of "The Red Wheelbarrow," which accompanies the poem as reprinted in William Rose Benét's *Fifty Poets: An American Auto-Anthology* (1933), is that the poem reflects a surcharge of emotion that attaches itself to an ordinary object, thereby elevating it temporarily to a position of prominence above its ordinary status:

> The wheelbarrow in question stood outside the window of an old negro's house on a back street in the suburb where I live. It was pouring rain and there were white chickens walking about in it. The sight impressed me somehow as about the most important, the most integral that it had ever been my pleasure to gaze upon. And the meter though no more than a fragment succeeds in portraying this pleasure flawlessly, even it succeeds in denoting a certain unquenchable exaltation—in fact I find the poem quite perfect.[11]

If it is true that Williams glimpsed the wheelbarrow during a lull in a medical emergency in which one of his young patients lay between life and death, the surcharge of emotion would seem to be explained in a fashion that the poem itself, by virtue of its aesthetic, chooses not to pursue.[12] In any case, whatever the circumstances of Williams' experience, it is certain that he regarded the objects seen as an adequate symbol of his depth of feeling, together with the rhythms of the phrases chosen to render those objects. That an uninstructed reader might find both the objects and the rhythms totally inadequate is of no particular consequence to the imagist who must insist on holding fast to the principles of his Emersonian faith. "If," Emerson assures us,

your subject do not appear to you the flower of the world at this moment, you have not rightly chosen it. No matter what it is, grand or gay, national or private, if it has a natural prominence to you, work away until you come to the heart of it: then it will, though it were a sparrow or a spider-web, as fully represent the central law and draw all tragic or joyful illustration, as if it were the book of Genesis or the book of Doom. (*CE*, VIII, 33–34)

It seems impossible to deny that imagism, thus explained, represents the fulfillment or the logical extension of an attitude embraced, even before Emerson's time, by the major romantic poets. Thus Keats, in a letter to Benjamin Bailey, observes that "probably every mental pursuit takes its reality and worth from the ardour of the pursuer—being in itself a nothing";[13] while Wordsworth, in explaining his seemingly trivial sonnet "With Ships the sea was sprinkled far and nigh" in a letter to Lady Beaumont, makes the crucial point that it is the thought and feeling *we* associate with objects that gives them their importance. Consequently, the ship that caught Wordsworth's attention to the extent that he "pursued her with a Lover's look" is worthy of a poem because it was the occasion of imaginative or mental activity on the part of the poet— and that activity alone has intrinsic value.[14] If Wordsworth had devoted his sonnet exclusively to a description of the ship that reportedly absorbed his attention, instead of telling the story of how his absorption came about, he might well have composed an imagist poem. Hegel too declares that the principle at stake here is central to romantic art, in which "purely external material," being "indifferent and vulgar" in itself, attains worth of its own only "if the heart has put itself into it and if it is to express not merely something inner but the heart's *depth of feeling.*"[15] The more successful the projection of the heart into the object, the more adequate the object as a term of expression. It remained, however, for the imagists in the twentieth century to eliminate the story, the forethought and afterthought, as something that had become ornamental or anecdotal, whose inclusion in the poem would lead to what Pound refers to as "work 'of second intensity.' "[16]

One does not expect to find in imagist poetry much in the way of overt reference to the poet, since such reference is excluded on principle. On the other hand, in poetry so resolutely bent on expressing the essence of the poet's subjectivity, one should expect to find (and indeed one does find) numerous hints or reminders of the poet's relationship to the things he images. In Williams' descriptions, certainly, there is often a considerable amount of pathetic fallacy, which reminds us that Williams has put his own emotional state into the things he is describing. In "Winter Quiet," for example, he observes that the trees "pirouette awkwardly" while the fences "watch" with "suppressed excitement" as the silver mist meets the bleached grass "Limb to limb, mouth to mouth" (*CEP*, 141) in act of sexual intimacy. In "Flowers by the Sea," chicory and daisies "seem hardly flowers alone / but color and the movement—or the shape / perhaps—of restlessness" (*CEP*, 87). In "The Botticellian Trees," there is a "song of the leaves" (*CEP*, 80); in "Wild Orchard," a tree with green and red apples is "a signal of finality / and perfect ease," while among a "savage / aristocracy of rocks" one rock "risen as a tree, / has turned / from his repose" (*CEP*, 88–89). The whole season is personified in Williams' celebrated poem "By the road to the contagious hospital." At first the spring is "sluggish" and "dazed," even a bit "uncertain," but soon the plants that manifest it begin to return one by one with "the stark dignity of / entrance," beginning, as Williams says, to "awaken" (*CEP*, 241–42). In "Spring Strains," the "blue-grey buds" are "erect with desire" (*CEP*, 159), while the trees in "The Trees" "thrash and scream / guffaw and curse" (*CEP*, 66). In "The Yachts," one of the most spectacular examples of pathetic fallacy occurs when Williams describes how the "moody" sea becomes "an entanglement of watery bodies" in the form of waves (or arms) "with hands grasping" which "seek to clutch at the prows" of the yachts (*CEP*, 106–07). There is nothing incidental about the device, either. It is absolutely fundamental to Williams' whole way of thinking, and examples of it, both serious and whimsical, are legion throughout his poetry. *Paterson*, for that matter, is a gigantic pathetic fallacy based on the assumption that any city may be regarded as the extended embodiment of a man, "all the de-

tails of which may be made to voice his most intimate convictions"
(*P*, 3). Thus the people of Paterson, New Jersey, are said to be the
"thoughts" of the giant N. F. Paterson (*P*, 18), while Williams'
own poetry is said to be an attempt to interpret the "voice" or
"speech" of the Falls, a speech that is paralleled in the inarticulate
(though, at the same time, curiously expressive) behavior that
comes pouring out of Paterson's citizens.

   Another way in which we are reminded of Williams himself, as
we read those poems that appear to rely mainly on objective descriptions, has to do with our awareness, upon reflection, of the
point of view or angle of vision from which the objects in question
are seen. Sometimes the arrangement or grouping of objects seems
so arbitrary or eccentric that the scene thereby constituted may be
said to exist only for the eye of the poet. Thus in "A Portrait of the
Times," "an old / squint-eyed woman" and two "W.P.A. men"
are brought into relation with each other solely by the will of the
poet, and not because they are the elements of a situation that is apparent to anyone but the poet. Only outside the scene, in the poet's
voyeuristic consciousness, do the three individuals constitute a
unity according to the perceived simultaneity of their actions. One
man, says Williams, "was pissing"

>   while the other
>   showed
>   by his red
>
>   jagged face the
>   immemorial tragedy
>   of lack-love
>
>   while an old
>   squint-eyed woman
>   in a black
>
>   dress
>   and clutching
>   a bunch of

            late chrysanthemums
            to her
            fatted bosoms

            turned her back
            on them
            at the corner
                  (*CEP*, 92)

Although the two men are presumably standing fairly close to each
other in a new "sluiceway // overlooking / the river," they are engaged in separate actions that would seem to occur on different lev-
els. One of them is pissing, while the other is showing the tragedy
of lack-love in his face. By describing these "actions" as though
they were taking place on the same ontological plane, Williams
quietly calls attention to his own action of bringing that which is
apparently unrelated into relation. Neither of the men is concerned
about the other, nor is it clear that the old woman who turns her
back on them at the corner has seen them or is conscious of them in
any way. Detached as they are from one another, each absorbed in
his or her own private world, the three form a tableau, a synthesis, for Williams alone. If a refusal to countenance what she has
glimpsed is implicit in the woman's turning her back, that only confirms, in its own way, the indifference or self-absorption implicit in
the act of pissing in public. Against the background of so much in-
attentiveness, we cannot help but feel a counterforce in the atten-
tive concern of Williams himself, who notices and binds together
what would otherwise remain unseen and fragmented.

    In "The Sun Bathers" (*CEP*, 457), we find a similar arrangement
of details composing a situation that exists only for the consciousness of the poet. The young man "begrimed / and in an old / army
coat" and the "fat negress" leaning out of a nearby window have no
particular relationship to each other of which either is conscious.
What holds them together is the fact that Williams can see both of
them simultaneously and can identify them, somewhat improbably
and humorously, as sunbathers. *He* determines the point of comparison, the point of contact, that the title makes explicit, just as he

determines which details shall stand out in relief and which shall remain submerged in "the conglomerate normality with which they are surrounded and of which before the act of 'creation' each is a part" (*SE*, 233).

In "View of a Lake" (*CEP*, 96–97), the scene is built up more slowly and in greater detail as Williams defines the context of three children who are looking intently into a lake and, at the same time, ignoring the traffic jam behind them in which Williams himself seems to be located as a temporarily idle driver taking in the view. The title of the poem may refer, however, to the children's view, since they are the ones who stand facing the water, bound together by a common interest in something Williams cannot see. Preoccupied as they are, the children stand "immobile in a line," forming the center of the panorama Williams takes in during his enforced idleness. The scene is a depressing one of urban-industrial ugliness, with cinders instead of grass, a railroad track with an iron post "planted" as though in defiant opposition to the single sycamore tree, a frame house "that looks / to have been flayed," and "the weed-grown / chassis / of a wrecked car." The reader is acutely aware that Williams' perception of these details is possible because he is temporarily unable to proceed about his business—this being an unanticipated, accidental moment of his mental life seemingly barren yet actually teeming with possibilities depending on the range and depth of his interest. The freedom he has to attend to one detail rather than another, to range widely or concentrate narrowly on that which lies before him, seems to be the essential condition of the experience related in the poem. Moreover, it is not unlikely that Williams' interest in the children is connected to their ability to focus their attention, just as he is focusing his attention on them. Thus the subject of the poem might well be the triumph that consciousness has always within its grasp despite the often depressing material conditions with which it must contend. Just as Williams has the power to find something interesting, something worthy of attention, in the most unlikely circumstances, so it is possible that by staring intently into the water the children are exercising a similar power, despite an environment that seems, from a conventional point of view, almost calculated to wear down their spirits and destroy their sensitivity. If such is the case, then their ability to ignore the traffic behind them and the ugliness around them (the conglomerate normality with which *they* are surrounded) is the counterpart of Williams' freedom.

Indeed, it is precisely this freedom that characterizes all of Williams' poems that have to do with his experience of the phenomenal world. To read them in bulk is to realize at once that Williams does not consider himself bound to observe any rules whatsoever regarding the observation and presentation of objects—not even imagist rules. Often he does pick out a single detail or a single thing in accordance with the imagist predilection for narrowly focused particulars, but just as frequently he draws back to enjoy a wider view, which results in the rapid summary of details found in poems like "Simplex Sigilum Veri" and "To Elsie." In truth, imagism may permit a narrow focus, but it does not prohibit the stringing together of numerous particular details so that any phase of experience may be rendered with as much simplicity or as much complexity as the poet happens to choose. One becomes aware, finally, that Williams' absorption in any one particular or group of particulars is conditioned by his freedom to withdraw himself out of them and to pass beyond them in a perfectly self-possessed, self-conscious transcendence. One of the clearest expressions of this freedom is found in the poem called "The Right of Way" from the *Spring and All* sequence. In this poem we are apprised of the "supreme importance" of a "nameless spectacle," which Williams encounters while driving down the road in his automobile. The lines describing the spectacle are almost sufficient to stand by themselves and might well have been introduced by the words "so much depends upon":

> an elderly man who
> smiled and looked away
>
> to the north past a house—
> a woman in blue

who was laughing and
leaning forward to look up

into the man's half
averted face

and a boy of eight who was
looking at the middle of

the man's belly
at a watchchain—
                    (*CEP*, 258)

The precision with which this fleeting aspect is described suggests
the degree to which Williams has attended to it—delighting in it as
an arrangement or composition of figures in a group. Yet the poem
is not primarily about the content of Williams' vision; it is about his
"right of way," the freedom he has to approach and depart from
such spectacles without impairing his essential independence. Thus
he speeds by the trio "without a word" and eventually encounters
another sight, equally important: "a girl with one leg / over the
rail of a balcony" (*CEP*, 259). This could go on forever, and, in a
sense, it does if we consider that reading through a large number
of Williams' poems is rather like riding along with him in the car,
moving from spectacle to spectacle (after the fashion of "January
Morning"), without once feeling he has compromised the self-
possession that makes such movement possible.

In fact, for every one of Williams' poems that limits itself to a
bare presentation of the facts, there are at least ten that do not.
These latter poems depict, more openly than the others, the intense
self-awareness Williams always maintains in his dealings with the
facts, whether he flaunts it or not. Quite often, as in "Smell!" or
"Pastoral" or "A Marriage Ritual," it is Williams himself who is
presented as the main character, enjoying things but also, at the
same time, keeping a delicate balance between involvement and
detachment—indeed, enjoying things in a special way *because of*
his detachment. In "The Thinker," we have a good example of the
voyeurism that gives so many of his poems their distinctive flavor.
There we see Williams admiring his wife's new pink slippers.
However, he does not give his poem over to the slippers them-

selves. Instead, having raised them by means of the pathetic fallacy to the level of autonomous creatures, he describes himself contemplating them and talking to them in his imagination. He admires the slippers from afar, partly because it is slightly absurd of him to do so but also because they are more delectable when enjoyed in secret. In his "secret mind" he talks to them "out of pure happiness" (*CEP*, 220). In poems like this, we observe Williams observing himself in the act of observing something else, and we see a man who relishes the fact that his imagination can attach whatever significance he pleases to the object of his interest. In "Danse Russe" and "Perfection" the intensity of Williams' feeling is grounded in the special relationship he has to the object he happens to be contemplating. In "The Young Housewife," the object is a young woman whom Williams finds attractive. Though he appears not to be acquainted with her, he has evidently seen her more than once standing by the curb in front of her house. Passing by in his car each morning, Williams thinks of her voyeuristically when she is not there to be seen, and, when she is there, he observes that she is "uncorseted" and compares her to a fallen leaf. Though he does not speak, he enjoys her in his secret mind, relishing a relationship that is one-sided and, therefore, private. The poem does not convey the impression that Williams is in any significant way restricted by "what actually impinges on the senses." What matters most is that Williams sees the young woman with his mind's eye as she "moves about in negligee behind / the wooden walls of her husband's house" (*CEP*, 136) and that he manipulates her in his imagination by comparing her to a fallen leaf.

It must be remembered that the important thing about imagism, as far as Williams was concerned, was not that it set up rules and prescriptions for the poetic treatment of particular things, but that it enabled him to deal directly with the material of his own experience without having to conform his poems to the rhetorical conventions of any previous tradition. Thus, while he clearly delighted in his freedom to embrace the self-imposed limits of bare presentation, he interpreted this freedom as the power to do whatever he pleased. In one poem he presents without comment; in another he lectures or rhapsodizes. Occasionally he eschews figurative expressions; more often he uses them flagrantly, in jest and in earnest. There is, therefore, no such thing as the "typical" Williams poem. Poems like "The Red Wheelbarrow" or "Between Walls" are certainly no more typical than "Dedication for a Plot of Ground" or "The Catholic Bells" or "The Old House." If in "The Pot of Flowers" he gives us a rapid, almost breathless description of the interrelationship of light, color, and form in a floral image that has been detached from the conglomerate normality, in "The Flower" he gives us a leisurely sequence of descriptions, judgments, and recollections strung together in a sort of stream of consciousness. The "flower" in this latter poem is purely metaphorical in that its petals are none other than the various strands of association which comprise Williams' experience of his city.

In short, if imagism suggests a rationale and a technique for dealing with those things that are immediately present to us, under our very noses, it also delivers us from "our fearful bedazzlement with some concrete and fixed present" (*SE*, 117–18), so that the senses do not have to see "a finality" when they witness "what is immediately before them in detail" (*I*, 14). By permitting us to reduce our experiences to elements or aspects which may then be recombined or juxtaposed to suit our own purposes, imagism not only frees us from the tyranny of the stereotype, it frees us as well from the content of immediate experience: "Thus a poem is tough by no quality it borrows from a logical recital of events *nor from the events themselves* but solely from that attenuated power which draws perhaps many broken things into a dance giving them thus a full being" (*I*, 16–17; italics added). It is by virtue of this power alone that the poet can "use anything at hand to assert himself. If he cannot do so he is less than great. The proof that I am I is that I can use anything, not a special formula but anything."[17] And so, by bringing the whole phenomenal world into subjection, Williams bears out the truth of Hegel's observation that the romantic artist, at the very end of art's development, must break away from the grip of objectivity in order to present himself as the true locus of value and meaning. "Bondage," says Hegel,

> to a particular subject-matter and a mode of portrayal suitable for this material alone are for artists today something past, and art therefore

has become a free instrument which the artist can wield in proportion
to his subjective skill in relation to any material of whatever kind. The
artist thus stands above specific consecrated forms and configurations
and moves freely on his own account, independent of the subject-
matter and mode of conception in which the holy and eternal was previously made visible to human apprehension. . . . The great artist
today needs in particular the free development of the spirit; in that development all superstition, and all faith which remains restricted to
determinate forms of vision and presentation, is degraded into mere
aspects and features. These the free spirit has mastered because he sees
in them no absolutely sacrosanct conditions for his exposition and
mode of configuration, but ascribes value to them only on the strength
of the higher content which in the course of his re-creation he puts into
them as adequate to them.[18]

Once the implications of imagism are grasped, it is easy to see
how Williams' second theory of poetry—the objectivist theory—
represents, at one and the same time, both the culmination of imagism and its annihilation; for if imagism manifests the poet's transcendence of the phenomenal world in and through the work of
art, objectivism manifests the same transcendence with respect to
the artwork itself. While imagism was instrumental in establishing
the poet's proper authority over things, it said little, Williams felt,
about the actual construction of poems. In one sense, of course, it
was perfectly true to say that the poet uses things to express himself—things seen and heard in the course of daily experience—but,
in another sense, it was not true. Sitting down to write, the poet
finds very quickly that his real materials are words. The problem
with imagism was that it seemed to focus all the attention on the
things imaged while substantially ignoring the reality of the poem
itself as a verbal construct. To remedy this deficiency, Williams
proposed that we concentrate our attention, not on the ghostly
presences of things absent, but on the "actual word stuff" (*SL*, 94)
of the poetry, the deployment of words on the page. As he explains
in his *Autobiography*, imagism's weakness was that it lacked "formal necessity" and thus presented merely "projected objectifica-
tions," whereas objectivism rightly insisted that the poem itself is
an object, "an object that in itself formally presents its case and its
meaning by the very form it assumes" (*A*, 264).

On the other hand, it is obvious that imagism prepares the way

for objectivism in that it divests the subject matter of poetry of intrinsic interest and shifts our attention to the manner in which the
poet has related himself to it. Once this shift has taken place, we
are ready to accept the idea that the superficial content of a poem
is arbitrary, a mere "PRETEXT for the REAL thing which is a new artistic form" (*SL*, 44). Thus it is not what the poet "*says* that counts
as a work of art, it's what he makes, with such intensity of perception that it lives with an intrinsic movement of its own to verify its
authenticity" (*SE*, 257). If imagism diverts us from the world as it
is supposed to be in itself to the world as it is actually experienced
by the poet, objectivism takes us one step further by diverting us
from the experienced world of the poet (from our point of view,
a rumor) to the created world of the poem, which we can experience directly for ourselves. It is, logically, the next step in a sequence of reductions, each of which brings the poet himself into
greater prominence: from the world in itself to the world he perceives, and from thence to the world he makes. In relation to this
last world especially—the "complete little universe" (*P*, 261) of
the individual poem—the poet is more clearly than ever a god,
whose power is felt in all the decisions that have resulted in the poem's being made as it is.

Unfortunately, it is easy to misunderstand what Williams means
when he says, by way of elucidating this second theory of poetry,
that words are things or that a poem itself is a thing or an object.
He does not mean that poems and words exist independently of
him in some sort of absolute, inviolable fashion, as modern realism
supposes. On the contrary, he means that they have the same kind
of radical dependence on him that all things have when they are
understood properly according to the perspective of idealism. The
declaration that words are things makes sense only if we recall that
things themselves are words, the correlatives or, as Williams says,
the "corollaries" (*EK*, 128) of the mind that thinks them. Words
and things are equally real because, as objects of consciousness,
they both have exactly the same status. The imagist poet properly
claims sovereignty over every natural fact he encounters, except
that, according to Williams, he tends to neglect the materials of his

own art, thereby inadvertently elevating them to a falsely transcendent position. The objectivist poet takes one step backward in
order to focus his attention squarely on these materials, relegating
them to a position alongside other things. He is then faced with a
new version of the problem faced by the imagist poet, for now it
is up to him to take control over language itself, making it if he
can the perfect instrument of his power and establishing thereby
an even higher sovereignty.

Like the imagist, who must reject all preconceptions of the
things he encounters in the course of his experience, the objectivist
must similarly reject, as far as he is able, all preestablished conventions that would govern his use of language. This means, in the first
place, a rejection of traditional poetic forms, which, because they
are the creations of others, can only be regarded as alien impositions. Coming down to us from the past, these forms represent "the
track of something" (EK, 93) that continues to develop in the living poet. Honored though they may be as previous expressions of
the spirit, they have nevertheless ceased to be the supreme need
of the spirit. To compose yet another ode, yet another sonnet,
yet another epic in blank verse, would be to deny one's own authority over the means of expression. Similarly, to use any linguistic
pattern, be it a stanza or a line, a sentence or a phrase, in a manner
that is clearly recognizable as conventional or customary, is to
make a tacit admission that one does not have language in all its
aspects totally under control. This, in turn, would mean that in the
contest which is always taking place between the poet and his materials, the materials have won by proving, in some way, recalcitrant. Therefore, it is up to the poet to be a man—to compose his
poem as thoroughly as possible so that, at every level, he can avoid
being imposed upon by the formalities and rules that are seemingly
inherent in his chosen medium.

As we have already seen, Williams admired up to a point the verbal experiments of his fellow modernists, especially the experiments of James Joyce and Gertrude Stein. While at times he com-
plained about the effects of their influence, he liked the audacity
with which the modernists set out to deform conventional usage,

shaping sentences, phrases, and even individual words (as in *Finnegans Wake*) in ways that were not only new but also idiosyncratic. To Williams, it meant that artists who had chosen to work with words were, in fact, successfully mastering their medium, making it responsive at every level to their own inclinations. Thus it was not Joyce's use of myth that caused Williams to admire *Ulysses;* it was his use of words in "some unapparent sequence quite apart from the usual syntactical one" (*SE,* 28). The presence of odd syntactical constructions could only mean, as far as Williams was concerned, that the novel was more thoroughly composed than novels that avoid such constructions. By this standard, of course, *Finnegans Wake* outdoes even *Ulysses,* representing an advance over the earlier novel's already outlandish techniques. Despite certain reservations,[19] Williams could not help but admire it as a sign of Joyce's nearly total victory over language:

Joyce's work in "Work in Progress" is the inevitable outcome of processes which he first realized in *Ulysses.* He has attacked the words themselves as the materials of letters—whereas Gertrude Stein has dealt mostly with their configurations—realizing that the intelligence is at a stop in them (as exemplified by the emotional and intellectual limits any one language puts upon the group using it—the stultification implied in the word "patriotism"). Thus his new work is infinitely superior to *Ulysses.* (*EK,* 17–18)

For similar reasons Williams also admired the way Pound worked with language in the *Cantos.* "He is seeking," says Williams in his review of *A Draft of XXX Cantos,* "to demonstrate the intelligence . . . by laboring with the material as it exists in speech and history" (*SE,* 110). The result of such labor is that the verse has "a faceted quality" that calls attention to itself. Each of the words stands out as "an objective unit in the design," making it obvious to the sensitive reader that all of them "have been used willingly by thought" (*SE,* 111). Thus it cannot be said that Pound is at the mercy of his medium, as many writers are. Instead, he whips it into shape, choosing "flawlessly where and what he will create" (*SE,* 110)—not with respect to "the sentiments, ideas, schemes portrayed" but "in the minute organization of the words and their relationships" (*SE,* 109).

It follows, I think, that it is not at all the aim of the objectivist to deny himself or to hide himself from the view of the reader. Quite the opposite, he expects to impress the reader mightily (as Williams was impressed by Joyce and Pound) by giving a virtuoso demonstration of what it really means to *use* language. If the imagist unfixes the land and the sea, making them revolve around the axis of his primary thought by disposing them anew, the objectivist does precisely the same thing with nouns, verbs, and adjectives. He disposes them anew so that everywhere his poem will reflect the fullness of his power. Romantic egoism is, therefore, unquestionably the basis of what Williams means by objectivism. *"It is not merely to make a thing* called a poem on a piece of paper that the poet is working," says Williams, "it is to permit feeling to BE by making a vehicle for it."[20] Indeed, the poem may be said to exist as an object for the sole purpose of enabling the poet to exist, and to manifest himself, as a thinking subject. That explains why Williams is so insistent in *Spring and All* that "in great works of the imagination A CREATIVE FORCE IS SHOWN AT WORK MAKING OBJECTS WHICH ALONE COMPLETE SCIENCE AND ALLOW INTELLIGENCE TO SURVIVE" (*I*, 112).

Presumably any poem that sets out to impress us by the strangeness of its constructions may be regarded as objectivist according to Williams' conception of objectivism. The poems in *Spring and All* are notoriously odd in this respect, and they have been compared to cubist paintings because of their tendency to combine perfectly ordinary words in unfamiliar sequences that refuse to coalesce in a single, coherent, determinate meaning.[21] Disdaining as they do the decorum of the English sentence, such poems as "Rigamarole" or "The Agonized Spires" are so wonderfully improbable in their combinations of words, so forbidding (or inviting) in their freedom from punctuation, that they are just on the verge of being unreadable. Confronted with the problem of reading them, most interpreters have found it convenient not to disentangle the sentiments, ideas, and schemes portrayed, but to consider instead why Williams wanted to entangle them in the first place. That is to say, they try to explain why Williams chose to use language in such a way as to produce thematic dislocations and entanglements. By directing our attention to the rationale that lies behind the poems dictating their verbal strategy, this kind of interpretation tends to confirm the conclusion that objectivist poems always have the same basic meaning in that they always mean the freedom they exhibit in their construction. In turn, this freedom confirms the fact that, as Hegel puts it, "the artist's subjective skill surmounts his material and its production because he is no longer dominated by the given conditions of a range of content and form already inherently determined in advance."[22]

Paterson is perhaps the best example of objectivism, for it is *Paterson*, above all, that reveals at every turn its status as a thoroughly composed and, therefore, thoroughly dependent object. More conspicuously than any other poem by Williams, *Paterson* is a mosaic or a collage of materials drawn from the most heterogeneous sources, including snippets of verse by Williams himself as well as lengthy quotations from books of fact and folklore, newspaper articles, and personal letters addressed to the author. To borrow a phrase from "The Agonized Spires," our first impression of the poem is that it is an "untamed aggregate" of miscellaneous pieces of verse and prose yoked together by violence. Subsequently, we realize that the point is precisely that the aggregate *has* been tamed, that the pieces *are* brought into relation by an act of will on the part of the poet. Strictly speaking, the final ordering of passages has little to do with the intrinsic nature of Williams' subject, which is ostensibly the moral history of Paterson. Despite the fact that certain motifs having to do with various aspects of the city recur frequently so that the poem has a certain degree of thematic consistency as well as structural sameness from section to section and book to book, the real unity of the poem is provided by Williams' own mind as it casts about among its materials, arranging them according to the principle of comparison and contrast. One element can always be related to another, and that in turn can be juxtaposed with something else—and so on to the end. It goes without saying, of course, that most of the material does have a bearing either on the moral dimensions of Paterson itself or on Williams' effort to make the city into a poem; but, in truth, anything can find a place in the poem so long as Williams happens to think about it. That, in fact, is the point. Anything—from a paragraph in John Addington Symonds' *Studies of the Greek Poets,* to a photograph of an African chief with his nine wives in *National Geographic Magazine,* to a survey of the geological material in the substrata beneath the city—anything can be alluded to, or described, or even reproduced verbatim (if it is part of a text), because everything in Williams' consciousness is potentially relevant to everything else in Williams' consciousness. Hence we feel quite rightly as we read through the whole of the poem that virtually any passage could be shifted from one location to another, that the quotations could be lengthened, shortened, or even dropped in any particular instance, indeed that the poem could be expanded, abridged, or edited in any number of ways without really altering its basic character or changing what it has to say. The one thing that matters—the law of free association, which Williams alludes to when he speaks of "the dance / of my thoughts" (*P,* 261)—would remain constant. By the term "free association," I do not mean to imply that *Paterson* was necessarily composed in a state of revery or that its parts were assembled haphazardly or spontaneously. I mean simply that Williams was evidently not constrained, either by the nature of his project or by the nature of his materials, to produce the order he did in fact produce. Instead, he was free to associate in any order of his choosing whatever presented itself to his consciousness. Notwithstanding the many helpful discussions of *Paterson* that have appeared in recent years, Randall Jarrell's famous definition of the poem's structure as an "organization of irrelevance" is still apt because it is based on the correct intuition that Williams himself is the real center of gravity.

The extent of Williams' power over the poem can be seen from the fact that he reserved the right to take things out and put things in at will. Thus the passage beginning with "The descent beckons" (from the third section of Book II) was later used as a separate poem in *The Desert Music and Other Poems,* while the poem entitled "Tribute to the Painters" from *Journey to Love* appears virtually intact in Book V. The implication is that any part of the whole of *Paterson* is also a whole, sufficient unto itself. Similarly, we can regard any other whole poem as at least potentially a part of the "complete" *Paterson*. In this way, the integrity of the poem is removed from the poem itself and placed at the discretion of the poet. As soon as Williams decided to extend the poem (which he did almost immediately after the publication of what was supposed to have been the fourth and final book), *Paterson* became again in fact what its structure indicated it always was in essence—a work in progress, fluid and indeterminate—and it remained so until Williams' death. The fixed Emersonian circle it threatened to be in four books, or even in five books, was thereby shattered so that the poem might become instead an ever-widening, ever-expanding circle, like the mind that produced it.

Indeed, the moral of *Paterson* is not just that "anything is good material for poetry" (*P*, 262) or that any subject is suitable as a pretext for a poem; the moral is that any disposition of verbal material *is* a poem, if a poet says it is. A poem is not a poem because it conforms to an external standard; it is a poem because, whatever it may look like and however it takes shape, it has been put forth as such by a poet. Largely for this reason, I would argue that *Paterson* exhibits an extreme form of what Hegel calls romantic humor, which is both an attitude and a method of organization appropriate to the artist who has completely transcended his materials. Such humor or wit is, as Hegel says, one of the signs of art's ultimate dissolution:

> Now humour is not set the task of developing and shaping a topic objectively and in a way appropriate to the essential nature of the topic, and, in this development, using its own means to articulate the topic and round it off artistically; on the contrary, it is the artist himself who enters the material, with the result that his chief activity, by the power of subjective notions, flashes of thought, striking modes of interpretation, consists in destroying and dissolving everything that proposes to make itself objective and win a firm shape for itself in reality, or that seems to have such a shape already in the external world. Therefore every independence of an objective *content* along with the inherently fixed connection of the *form* (given as that is by the subject-matter) is annihilated in itself, and the presentation is only a sporting with topics,

a derangement and perversion of the material, and a rambling to and fro, a criss-cross movement of subjective expressions, views, and attitudes whereby the author sacrifices himself and his topics alike.[23]

By way of illustration, Hegel offers a description of one of his own contemporaries, the novelist J. P. F. Richter (better known as Jean Paul), but the description he gives is also applicable to the procedures of many modernist writers. Reading it, one cannot help but think of *Paterson* or the *Cantos*, perhaps even *Finnegans Wake* or *The Waste Land*—each, in its own way, a monument of romantic egoism disguised as an exercise in "impersonality" and "objectivity":

So with us Jean Paul, e.g., is a favourite humourist, and yet he is astonishing, beyond everyone else, precisely in the baroque mustering of things objectively furthest removed from one another and in the most confused disorderly jumbling of topics related only in his own subjective imagination. The story, the subject-matter and course of events in his novels, is what is of the least interest. The main thing remains the hither and thither course of the humour which uses every topic only to emphasize the subjective wit of the author. In thus drawing together and concatenating material raked up from the four corners of the earth and every sphere of reality, humour turns back, as it were, to symbolism where meaning and shape likewise lie apart from one another, except that now it is the mere subjective activity of the poet which commands material and meaning alike and strings them together in an order alien to them. But such a string of notions soon wearies us, especially if we are expected to acclimatize ourselves and our ideas to the often scarcely guessable combinations which have casually floated before the poet's mind.[24]

It is almost certain that Hegel, an admirer of classical art, would have deplored the methods of Pound and Williams, not to mention those of Joyce and Eliot, but at least he would have been able to identify them correctly. He would have seen at once that the method of witty juxtaposition with little or no commentary—the method so central to the principal works of modernism—is merely a continuation or extension of romantic humor, one more sign of the victory of inwardness over the external. Clearly the following remarks, again having to do with Jean Paul, seem uncannily prophetic with respect to the major figures of modern poetry:

Jean Paul's humour often surprises us by its depth of wit and beauty of feeling, but equally often, in an opposite way, by its grotesquely combining things which have no real connection with one another, and the relations into which his humour brings them together are almost indecipherable. Even the greatest humourist has not relations of this kind present in his memory and so after all we often observe that even Jean Paul's interconnections are not the product of the power of genius but are brought together externally. Thus in order always to have new material, Jean Paul looked into books of the most varied kind, botanical, legal, philosophical, descriptive of travel, noted at once what struck him and wrote down the passing fancies it suggested; when it was a matter of actual composition, he brought together the most heterogeneous material—Brazilian plants and the old Supreme Court of the Empire. This is then given special praise as originality or as humour by which anything and everything is excused. But such caprice is precisely what true originality excludes.[25]

Hegel goes on in this passage to speak contemptuously of a form of irony that "likes to pass itself off as the highest originality," and, in doing so, he describes almost exactly the modern method of showing the things themselves in action without benefit of explicit assertion. One aspect of this irony, says Hegel, is that

it brings together in its representations a mass of external details, the inmost meaning of which the poet keeps to himself. Then the cunning and loftiness of this procedure is supposed to consist in enlarging the imagination on the ground that precisely in these collocations and external details there lie concealed the 'poetry of poetry' and everything most profound and excellent, which, purely and simply because of its depth, cannot be expressed. So, e.g., in F. von Schlegel's poems at the time when he imagined himself a poet, what is unsaid is given out as the best thing of all; yet this 'poetry of poetry' proved itself to be precisely the flattest prose.[26]

What is this "poetry of poetry" but another name for the implicit meaning the imagist and the objectivist both seek to convey by means of cunning arrangements of things used as words or words used as things? Art for both kinds of poet is essentially "a matter of concrete indirections" (*SL*, 24), and so what really matters is "the thing I have intimated if not expressed" (*SL*, 26), "the thing I cannot quite name" (*A*, 288).

Somehow, curiously, Hegel foresaw this whole development, or rather he described the seeds of it in the literature of his own time and place. He understood that the poetry of things, with its collocations of external details, was not founded on a permanent rapprochement between mind and world, or between the human spirit and the natural fact. Rather he knew it was based on the ever-widening gulf between them, caused by the mind's discovery of its own preeminence. Emerson, we observe, does not call for a poetry *of* the land and sea; he calls for a poetry that *unfixes* land and sea—making them revolve around the axis of the poet's own thought. Similarly, in his memoir of Gaudier-Brzeska, Pound tells us not that great works of art are identical with fact but that they are "lords over fact."[27] In *Paterson*, Williams exercises his lordship by making the facts assume a new position as the elements of a new syntax. Each of the passages selected for quotation (and each passage of original poetry as well) becomes a "word" in the elaborate "assertion" that the poem keeps building, section by section and book by book, without ever reaching a conclusion. Even the Mike Wallace interview, which in its original location reads like a contemptuous and largely successful attack on Williams ("Mike Wallace Asks William Carlos Williams Is Poetry A Dead Duck"), is eventually mastered and pressed into service as one of Williams' "words" in the syntactical arrangement of passages that constitutes *Paterson Five*. Indeed, because of its new location in the poem, Williams gets the last laugh by tacitly confirming the point he makes during the interview that anything, including a newspaper column, is good material for poetry. Surely it is this kind of ingenuity that *Paterson* chiefly expresses, not the environment, which in itself is merely the occasion of ingenuity. What Williams says of Pound, then, we may say of Williams: "He is seeking to demonstrate the intelligence . . . by laboring with the material as it exists in speech and history" (*SE*, 110).

Nevertheless, if imagism proves to be somewhat less than satisfactory, so does objectivism, in the final analysis. Even the thoroughly composed, obviously constructed verbal object—the poem as a "thing" or as a mosaic of "things"—must finally fail to give an adequate demonstration of the nature and form of intelligence be-

cause it is only *the effect* of intelligence. Though it rightly empha-
sizes the fact that a poem is the product or result of spiritual activity, in doing so it freezes the spirit in one particular shape, so that
it remains, in that shape, fixed and unchanging. As an effect of
spirit, the objectivist poem is truly admirable and worthy of contemplation, just as the works of God are similarly admirable and
worthy to be contemplated; as an image of spirit, however, it is
misleading because it is lifeless, whereas spirit is life itself. From
the point of view of the poet who is actively engaged in producing
a work, the tractableness or malleability of "actual word stuff" is
useful in that it helps to establish, by contrast, the opposite principle of his own free vitality. On the other hand, from the point of
view of him who surveys a work, it is clear that the spirit which
produced it is belied by its own product. In the process of being
constructed, the poem at hand achieves a momentary eminency
for the poet (as it does for the reader also in the immediate act of
interpretation). It is, or it seems to be, precisely what the poet has
in his mind to say. As soon as he finishes it, though, the poem becomes "perfectly blank to him" (*SE*, 56) because it is no longer
what he has in his mind to say. It is an Emersonian circle that ceases
to be the supreme need of the spirit as soon as it is drawn: "Now I
am not what I was when the word was forming to say what I am"
(*I*, 158). What is the objectivist poem, after all, but a formal pattern, and what are formal patterns but "arrests of the truth in some
particular phase of its mutations" (*SE*, 205), "the track of something which has passed" (*EK*, 93)? In contemplating even the
greatest of the imagination's works, "we are left staring at the
empty casings where truth lived yesterday while the creature itself has escaped behind us" (*SE*, 213).

However important it may be to embody the truth in a particular shape or form, it is equally important to escape or transcend
particular embodiments by identifying them as that which stands
in opposition to the truth. For this reason, Williams' objectivist
definition of a poem as "a small (or large) machine made of words"
(*SE*, 256) cannot be understood apart from his repeated assertion
that the purpose of writing is precisely to liberate oneself and oth-

ers from the idolatry of machinery. An artist writes, according to
Williams, "to assert himself above every machine and every me-
chanical conception that seeks to bind him."[28] In *The Embodiment
of Knowledge*, he makes this point especially clear:

As soon as we make [the machine] we must at once plan to escape—and
escape. By this we understand the escape of man from domination by
his own engines. Thus continually he asserts himself above what he
knows and which has tended to fix him as part of itself. To stop before
any machine is to make of it a fetish attended by its metaphysical priest
the engineer. (*EK*, 62–63)

But what if it were possible to invent a form that was capable of
reflecting the process of mutation itself, a form that did not "arrest"
the truth but instead allowed it to unfold in its own true shape as
that which is beyond shape? What a paradox that would be! A formal solution to the problem of form itself, a form that would permit feeling to be and, at the same time, represent the complete triumph of subjectivity over its own manifestation. This, ultimately,
is the goal of Williams' third theory of poetry, which dominates
the last phase of his development. Was there a device that would
allow him to represent not the objects of thought but thought itself
in its truth as a temporal process? Increasingly, this seemed to him
to be the only thing that really mattered—not the facts, nor even
the creation of verbal objects which in themselves are only means
to an end, but rather the discovery of a device for capturing the
rhythms of actual speech in which Williams believed he could
detect the very life of our secret mind. In the new measure, he
hoped to find at last the perfectly adequate embodiment of the
formless truth.

We cannot even begin to appreciate the significance of Williams' third theory of poetry unless we see that this is what the new
measure is supposed to accomplish. It is not simply a matter of
learning to combine words in groups that move at the same pace
despite the fact that they contain different numbers of syllables. It
is a matter of establishing flexible patterns of rhythm in which can
be heard the authentic movements of the spirit within us, patterns
that enable our utterances to become more plainly its utterance.[29]

In terms of the program he sketches in "Love and Service," we can
see how Williams might judge his new measure to be the ultimate
means of effecting our reconciliation with the unknown, for, in the
act of using it, we consciously become vehicles of "the mystery
about which nothing can be said"—not what we see or what we
make but we ourselves in the speech that wells up from within us.
Having made all things subordinate to himself by virtue of the
techniques associated with imagism and objectivism, Williams has
only one thing left to do—he has to make himself subordinate to the
spirit by allowing it to imprint itself or impose itself on the movement of his verses. When that happens, the spirit will be all-in-all
in his poetry—the only thing of importance—displacing every other
interest.

Thus, in spite of his hostility toward the more conventional
modes of symbolism, Williams' new measure is really the ultimate
symbol, for it combines all interests in one and promises to be at
least in principle the last form we shall ever need, being the embodiment of change itself, the form of formlessness. In his essay "How
to Write," Williams explains how the rhythms of poetry may
originate in and reflect the deeper aspects of mind which are universal rather than individual. Good writing, he says, begins only
when the writer lets go of his inhibitions and allows himself to
write so spontaneously that he touches "a primitive profundity of
the personality":

The faculties, untied, proceed backward through the night of our unconscious past. It goes down to the ritualistic, amoral past of the race, to
fetish, to dream to wherever the "genius" of the particular writer finds
itself able to go. (*IWCW*, 97)

The writer becomes, in this manner, a conduit of the mind's "demonic power," tapping the true source of his own particular
genius:

The demonic power of the mind is its racial and individual past, it is
the rhythmic ebb and flow of the mysterious life process and unless
this is tapped by the writer nothing of moment can result. It is the reason for the value of poetry whose unacknowledged rhythmic symbolism is its greatest strength and which makes all prose in comparison
with it little more than the patter of the intelligence. (*IWCW*, 98)

Here, then, is the key to the real significance of the new measure—
an "unacknowledged rhythmic symbolism" that reflects "the
rhythmic ebb and flow of the mysterious life process." We are not
to suppose, however, that in referring to the "life process," Williams is attempting to explain art naturalistically in terms of human
physiology. Indeed, the ebb and flow of the life process, which he
mentions here, may very well refer to the mysterious love described in "Love and Service" which "is not anything mortal" and
which "flows over the forms of the world like water that comes
and withdraws" (EK, 184). In other words, Williams is not making biochemistry the basis of art, "for, living, as with truth, is also a
thing without a body and expressed here merely" (EK, 182).

To the extent that we make contact with this "primitive profundity of the personality," we find our proper place. "Place" in
Williams' lexicon is not only nor even primarily a physical location,
like London or Paris. It is first of all "a certain position of the understanding anterior to all systems of thought, as well as of fact
and of deed" (EK, 132):

> It is the past, (from which man has come). It is the "night mind," the
> chaos, the source of religion; the preconscious, the savage, the animal,
> the plant, the inorganic—what you will.
> But it is none of these. It is one: all tentatives fit into it, not it into
> them. It is particularly not "the past" out of which knowledge or con-
> sciousness going "up" proceeds, leaving it behind. It exists co-inciden-
> tally with consciousness, systems, is not escaped. (EK, 133)

To the extent that he touches this primitive, original depth within
himself, the writer reaches that which is "common to all" (EK,
132), that upon which "everything else rests, every action, thought,
system" (EK, 133). Since it is potentially discernible in every
spontaneous use of language, it is present also in the speech of others to whom the writer eagerly listens in an effort to detect the
"natural sense of measure" that lies at the heart of language, consti-
tuting "its deepest truth":

> It is there that poetry meets the race. It is essentially different in En-
> glish and American. The poet's business is to find that basis, to discover
> it in the speech around him and to build it into his compositions.[30]

In all of this, we see Williams modifying the personal egoism that dominates his earlier theories of poetry. In his reflections on the new measure, the poet's ego is expanded until it becomes identical with the mind of the community, the American mind reflected in the American idiom. And that mind, in turn, is identified with a universal mind, a universal spirit, which has always existed everywhere in all. "All places," says Williams, "are alike to the spirit, all races become one and all continents the abode of a universal spirit."[31] It follows, as far as Williams is concerned, that

it is our duty as Americans, our devotional duty, let's say, to take out the spirit that has made not only Greek and Latin and French but British poetry also, and which restricts us when we're too stern about following their modes, and put it into something which will be far more liberating to the mind and the spirit of man. (*IWCW*, 26)

Williams' pursuit of the new measure must surely be the high-water mark of American transcendentalism, for it carries with it the assumption that our mere acknowledgment of the rhythmic symbolism of ordinary speech must coincide with and even effect a profound revolution in human affairs. "Is it inconceivable," Williams asks, "that in a single line, in a single poem the world can be shattered to bits?"[32] Perhaps, but it is true nonetheless. That is why Williams kept trying to locate what he called the "primary particles" or the "elementary particles" of which poetry is made.[33] By wielding such particles, he could make us whole again; he could make us grasp the principle of freedom itself by giving us a picture of it in the structure of his verses. Indeed, it is impossible to exaggerate the symbolic significance Williams attached to the new measure. As the very icon of iconoclasm, it seemed to him to represent a new spirit of liberation working in all spheres of activity, not just in that of the poem. The dogmatism of science for example, was being disturbed successfully by Einstein's theory of relativity, which confirmed, Williams thought, his own view that men lord it over the facts simply by measuring them. Very well, then, if science itself was beginning to accept the conclusion that man is "the judge of all his own activities" (*EK*, 133), what better way to represent this new wave of enlightenment than by using the "variable" or "relatively stable" foot?

How can we accept Einstein's theory of relativity, affecting our very conception of the heavens about us of which poets write so much, without incorporating its essential fact—the relativity of measurements—into our own category of activity: the poem. (*SE*, 283)

Was the spirit of American democracy sweeping over the world with the promise of liberty and abundance for all? If so, then why would any one still wish to write accentual verse? In a speech before the National Institute of Arts and Letters, Williams cited Toynbee's observation that our own age would be remembered as the first age in history in which it was thought to be both practicable and desirable to make the benefits of civilization available to the whole human race, and he went on to suggest that American poets could participate in and reflect this revolution in their poetry:

The basic idea which underlies our art must be, for better or worse, that which Toynbee has isolated for us: abundance, that is, permission, for all. And it is in the *structure* of our works that this must show. We must embody the principle of abundance, of total availability of materials, freest association in the measure, in *that* to differ from the poem of all previous time. It will be that sort of thing, if we succeed, that shall give us our supreme distinction. (*ARI*, 217–18)

Although at times it appeared that a revolution in consciousness was taking place anyway, whether or not it was being reflected in poetry, Williams clung stubbornly to the idea that it had to occur as well in the structure of poetry or else it would certainly miscarry. Poetry could make the crucial difference, he insisted to Thirlwall in 1955:

If the measurement itself is confined, every dimension of the verse and all implications touching it suffer confinement and generate pressures within our lives which will blow it and us apart. It is no matter that we are dealing with a comparatively unnoticed part of the field of our experience, the field of poetics, the result to our minds will be drastic. You cannot break through old customs, in verse or social organization, without drastically changing the whole concept and also the structure of our lives all along the line. (*SL*, 332)

Thus the new measure is more than just a reflection of consciousness that we can perhaps do without; it is the container, the shaper, of consciousness, which "lets more in, very specially, of the *present* spectacle of the world" while, at the same time, it "lets in the moods of our present life, which thus presented (in a poem) are real to us"—"It's got to do all that if we are to live and feel and be in our own location as we are, and know that the earth and the universe are ours."[34] No wonder then that during his last years Williams came to believe that almost everything of importance hinged on the discovery of this mystical measure.

The irony, of course, is that he never found it. Despite his "few experiments" in the 1950s, it remained undiscovered and merely potential. "Without invention," Williams wrote in *Paterson Two*, "nothing is well spaced" (*P*, 65); but in 1954 he was still complaining that "the construction of our poems . . . is left shamefully to the past" (*SE*, 337). "Shame on our poets," he declares in "Deep Religious Faith": "They have quit the job / of invention" (*PB*, 96). In 1955, he continued his denunciation: "The modernists who break their verses into convenient patterns of often incomprehensible jumbles of too abrupt transitions of the sense forget that in all they write the foot remains unaltered" (*SL*, 335). Even his own step-down or triadic line, which he deployed in *The Desert Music* and in *Journey to Love*, is modified considerably, when it is not abandoned, in his last volume, *Pictures from Brueghel*. Moreover, he made it clear in an interview with Walter Sutton in 1961 that he was still engaged in his search. "At the present time," he told Sutton, "I have been trying to approach a shorter line which I haven't quite been able to nail. I wanted the shorter line, the sparer line, and yet I want to give a measured line, but the divisions of the line should be shorter" (*IWCW*, 39). The irony, then, is that Williams could never really find an adequate embodiment of the measure that was, by definition, the perfect embodiment of what he had it in his mind to say. The spirit, which was to find its unique artistic representation—even, perhaps, its very existence—in "a new and hitherto neglected because virtually unknown measure,"[35] remains unknown because it remains "hidden" in every phrase we utter.

The climax of the third, and last, of Williams' three theories of poetry is that poetry itself has disappeared. It has been refined and compressed and reduced right out of existence. Poetry is, at last, the slain Osiris, and Williams is the Isis of the Pure Search. The whole world, formerly the subject of those "gaudy fables" deplored by Emerson, has been contracted to an image, narrowed to a point, and, finally, exploded into nothingness by being resolved into a matter not even of particles but of spaces—"spaces in between the various spaces of the verse" (*IWCW*, 39). What are we to make of this rather astonishing feat of prestidigitation? What does it mean? For one thing, it means that at the very end of his career Williams presents himself before "the great altar of the Unknown" with admittedly inadequate offerings, as he predicted in "Love and Service":

He tries to sing, he tries to dance, to speak praises in accordance with that which he sees but, of course, fails. The point however is that he tried to do a thing which had he been able he would have done. (*EK*, 180)

But this, in turn, only means that Williams fulfills his obligation to the Unknown by demonstrating again and again that it always sublimely exceeds its own representations. He does this by continually placing himself in a position of absolute authority: first, with respect to the poem as image; then, with respect to the poem as object; and, finally, with respect to the poem as rhythm sample. Undoubtedly, then, in all three of its forms, his art achieves a continual demonstration of the inadequacy of art by means of art. It represents, to use Hegel's terminology, "the self-transcendence of art but within its own sphere and in the form of art itself."[36] Facts, objects, speech rhythms—all these things come before us in Williams' poetry in such a way as to yield "the poetry of poetry"; but in every instance they point beyond themselves to a mind that has become so self-conscious it has learned to "conceive itself as standing beyond its processes" (*EK*, 42) and consequently knows itself to be "*outside* all categories" (*EK*, 52). Thus, in its truth, Williams' poetry conforms not only to his own prediction in "Love and Service" but also to Hegel's definition of romantic art in the *Aesthetics*, the entire content of which art, says Hegel,

is concentrated on the inner life of the spirit, on feeling, ideas, and the mind which strives after union with the truth, seeks and struggles to generate and preserve the Divine in the subject's consciousness, and now may not carry through aims and undertakings in the world for the sake of the world but rather has for its sole essential undertaking the inner battle of man in himself and his reconciliation with God; and it brings into representation only the personality and its preservation along with contrivances towards this end.[37]

The contrivances of Williams' art are the images, objects, and speech rhythms he uses to reconcile himself with "the mystery about which nothing can be said."

As it happens, however, Williams did not conform entirely to the principles laid down in his three theories of poetry, and for this we can be thankful. Each of his theories, as we have seen, requires that the poet use a method of "concrete indirection" in order to imply the reality of mind. In imagism, the description of a particular set of related (or unrelated) objects is supposed to imply the mind that perceives them or describes them. In objectivism, the construction of an object is supposed to imply the mind laboring with its verbal materials. In poetry committed to the mythology of a new measure, the rhythmic flow of properly paced syllables is supposed to imply the process of thought itself—the mutation of thought, the life of thought. But, for this last demonstration to occur, it is necessary that Williams actually think or, at least, give the appearance of thinking. Mere descriptions will hardly suffice, nor will crazy mosaics of words and passages, however much they put it up to the reader "to be a man." Poems that present the mere products of thought, the results of thought, are not nearly so effective in this respect as poems in which the poet simply takes upon himself the task of thinking, which is precisely what Williams does in the poetry of his last productive decade. Particularly in his poems of the early and middle 1950s, Williams shows himself to have been one of our greatest poets of meditation. Art as a matter of concrete indirections becomes so tenuous, so airy, when it is finally reduced to nothing but spaces in between spaces, that we are left primarily with the spectacle of Williams himself—thinking, feeling, and generally mulling over whatever happens to interest or concern him. Indeed, the techniques of indirection or self-alienation are so much less important in these later poems than they are in Williams' earlier poetry, it almost seems that art itself no longer matters as much as thinking about art or, in fact, thinking about anything. If there was ever an art that gave the appearance of having transcended art, it is the art of these poems.

5   Thinking as Salvation

Man is an animal, but even in his animal functions, he is not confined to the implicit, as the animal is; he becomes conscious of them, recognizes them, and lifts them, as, for instance, the process of digestion, into self-conscious science. In this way man breaks the barrier of his implicit and immediate character, so that precisely because he *knows* that he is an animal, he ceases to be an animal and attains knowledge of himself as spirit.

    —HEGEL, *Aesthetics*

Being able to estimate, to esteem, that is, to act in accordance with the standard of Being, is itself creation of the highest order.

    —HEIDEGGER, *Nietzsche*

In Williams' poetry of the 1950s, the center of interest is still, as much as it ever was, the mental or spiritual power of the poet. The only difference is that it stops being merely the covert subject and becomes the explicit subject as well. Instead of pouring himself outward into things (which can then be presented as the objective correlatives of his own consciousness), Williams withdraws into himself to contemplate things from a distance. In doing so, however, he necessarily cancels or raises to a higher level that immediate union with the world which is the tacit basis of his earlier poetry. Henceforth, it is thinking alone that must be regarded as supremely important, not wheelbarrows or sycamore trees which are but the occasions and products of thought. It is the thinker who now comes before himself, having been made the explicit subject of his own meditations, as Williams indicates in "The Descent."

"The descent beckons / as the ascent beckoned" (*PB*, 73), says Williams at the beginning of his final phase, and he means by this a descent into memory, a descent into his own inner depths, wherein he finds compensation for the increasingly disturbing poverty of that which is revealed by the senses. Like Wordsworth at the Simplon Pass, Williams reaches a point at which the external world no longer seems to provide an adequate correlative for his desires and expectations. His only recourse is to turn inward, as Wordsworth does, in search of satisfactions which the outward world apparently denies. The reasons for this change of direction are, in Williams' case, fairly obvious: the heart attack in 1948, the death of his mother in 1949, and, most spectacularly, the series of crippling strokes in 1951 and 1952 that almost completely knocked him out, paralyzing his right arm and seriously impairing his speech and eyesight. At this most critical time in his life, when the light of sense was almost permanently extinguished, he was forced to acknowledge "what we cannot accomplish, what // is denied to love, / what we have lost in the anticipation" (*PB*, 74). Up to this point, his lordship over the facts had never been seriously threatened; he had simply appropriated whatever he wanted, bending it to his will like a god. Now the whole world seemed to be threat-

ened with dissolution. The facts were becoming recalcitrant, in-
imical. They were "the sorry facts" (*PB*, 126), betokening "ruin
for myself / and all that I hold / dear" (*PB*, 90), and the question
was, what to do about it, how to respond. It was a genuine crisis for
Williams' idealism, but he met it characteristically and, as it turned
out, successfully by using the facts as an impetus to his own thinking. The drama of consciousness—the oyster's fretting over the
grain of sand—remained just as important as it had been, only now
it began to appear as a topic worthy of contemplation in its own
right. Indeed, Williams began to display it more directly in his
poetry than ever before, as he came to realize that the process of
constructing answers to the problems posed by death and dissolution was itself the answer he was seeking.

"The Descent" establishes a pattern often repeated in Williams'
later poetry; Williams takes the facts as he finds them and interprets them in such a way as to give them a new, more beneficent
character. The facts in themselves are neither disguised nor altered,
but Williams makes it possible for us to see them in a new way and
to give them new names. As a result, the problems they pose appear
to have been dissolved, while Williams himself appears to have
been elevated to a life of the spirit in which he is inwardly more
secure than ever before. With even greater assurance than before,
he demonstrates that, as Hegel writes in the *Phenomenology*,

the life of Spirit is not the life that shrinks from death and keeps itself
untouched by devastation, but rather the life that endures it and maintains itself in it. It wins its truth only when, in utter dismemberment, it
finds itself. It is this power, not as something positive, which closes its
eyes to the negative, as when we say of something that it is nothing or
is false, and then, having done with it, turn away and pass on to something else; on the contrary, Spirit is this power only by looking the
negative in the face, and tarrying with it. This tarrying with the negative is the magical power that converts it into being.[1]

In certain respects, the procedure Williams adopts for dissolving
the recalcitrance of the facts by interpreting them in a new way
also has an affinity with the meditative procedures of Wittgenstein,
who likewise makes philosophical problems disappear by showing
us how to reconceive them according to a new aspect. Wittgenstein's account of this method, as he explained it in a lecture at

Cambridge, is, therefore, helpful in understanding Williams' use
of it. Wittgenstein says,

What I give is the morphology of the use of an expression. I show that
it has kinds of uses of which you had not dreamed. In philosophy one
feels *forced* to look at a concept in a certain way. What I do is to suggest, or even invent, other ways of looking at it. I suggest possibilities
of which you had not previously thought. You thought that there was
one possibility, or only two at most. But I made you think of others.
Furthermore, I made you see that it was absurd to expect the concept
to conform to those narrow possibilities. Thus your mental cramp is
relieved, and you are free to look around the field of use of the expression and to describe the different kinds of uses of it.[2]

In "The Descent" Williams finds a similar way of looking at defeat
and loss that enables him to see those negative experiences as positive ones with implications not yet "realized." For example, it
occurs to him, as it also occurred to Wordsworth in an analogous
predicament, that the compensation for being dispossessed of the
world of the scenes is to be repossessed of it as it exists in the mind,
stored in memory. To be in full possession of the sensory world in
an immediate way, like an animal, is to be unwittingly in a state of
dispossession with respect to "the invisible world," which is available only to the "inward eye" of contemplation or reflection. Having reached this conclusion, Williams has the power to regard
what appears to be the end of life as, instead, "an initiation." What
was formerly his but now seems lost, i.e., the life of the senses, gives
way to that which was formerly "unsuspected" but is now his.
Williams accomplishes an impressive feat in thus transforming the
negative into something positive, but in so doing he merely reveals
another aspect of what he himself had said years before in "Love
and Service." When the "perishable signs" are destroyed, when
the forms of things are shattered (including the forms of our own
bodies), then "the permanent shines out for the first time clearly"
and "we see at last that love is not anything mortal." In "The
Descent," the truth of this prophetic observation is simultaneously
revealed and reasserted:

> With evening, love wakens
>   though its shadows
>   which are alive by reason

                    of the sun shining—
                            grow sleepy now and drop away
                                    from desire

            Love without shadows stirs now
                    beginning to awaken
                            as night
            advances.

                                                    (*PB*, 73–74)

    Williams' procedure in "The Descent" bears comparison with
Wittgenstein's procedure because what Williams does in that
poem is to take the *concept* of failure or defeat and show that it is
absurd to expect the concept to conform to the narrow possibilities it initially suggests. Memory, too, is also a *concept* that Williams teases and probes in the opening lines of the poem:

                            Memory is a kind
            of accomplishment,
                    a sort of renewal
                            even
            an initiation, since the spaces it opens are new places
                    inhabited by hordes
                            heretofore unrealized,
            of new kinds—
                    since their movements
                            are toward new objectives
            (even though formerly they were abandoned).

                                                    (*PB*, 73)

The point, of course, is that thinking about a previous experience
is not a matter of simply rehashing it or copying it over again in
thought. Instead it is a matter of having a new experience with the
same degree of risk or adventure that pertains to all experiences.
But the effect of the poem itself is to suggest that Williams is
slowly feeling his way toward this conclusion, looking for the
right term or the right comparison to elucidate the depth of meaning that the word "memory" comprises. The failure of immediate

experience to continue to be the unproblematic embodiment of his own inwardness entails for Williams a "descent" into memory, a retracting of previous steps. What then does memory entail? How does retracing previous steps accomplish something new? Memory makes possible the opening up of all concepts, including those of memory itself and failure. If Williams can conceive of memory in such a way that it seems to involve "accomplishment," "renewal," and even "initiation," if he can understand that "the descent" is both a reversal and a continuation of "the ascent" ("The descent beckons / as the ascent beckoned."), then indeed he can also grasp that failure, like memory, is similarly "inhabited by hordes" of implications "heretofore unrealized." His mental cramp is relieved because he is no longer obliged to suppose that memory, failure, or any other concept has only one meaning. Ultimately, "The Descent" makes it clear that the inadequacy of immediate experience is not primarily a factual problem; rather it is a conceptual problem to which a poem may be offered as a solution.

Williams makes use of his problem-solving technique in such poems as "To Daphne and Virginia." There the problem is his difficulty articulating the love he feels for his daughters-in-law, a difficulty caused in part by his infirmity but also by the ambiguity of his feeling. Above all, he feels the need to express himself with absolute clarity—the need to define his situation so precisely that there can be no mistake about the nuances of its implications. He begins by setting the problem:

> The smell of the heat is boxwood
> > when rousing us
> > > a movement of the air
> stirs our thoughts
> > that had no life in them
> > > to a life, a life in which
> two women agonize:
> > to live and to breathe is no less.
> > > Two young women.
> The box odor
> > is the odor of that of which

                        partaking separately,
        each to herself
            I partake also
                    · · separately.
                        (*PB*, 75)

The boxwood odor is important because it stimulates thought and
because it represents something that the poet has in common with
the two young women. But this is only a beginning. The life of
which he becomes conscious is a life of agony, and those who smell
the boxwood do so separately, in isolation. Somehow this isolation
and distress must be mitigated or overcome, yet Williams cannot
proceed in a physical way with a physical gesture. He must do it
spiritually or mentally through the medium of his poetry. Sexual
activity is out of the question for a number of reasons, but "the
mind's labors" are still available to him:

        Be patient that I address you in a poem,
                there is no other
                        fit medium.
        The mind
                lives there. It is uncertain,
                        can trick us and leave us
        agonized. But for resources
                what can equal it?
                        There is nothing. We
        should be lost
                without its wings to
                        fly off upon.

        The mind is the cause of our distresses
                but of it we can build anew.
                        Oh something more than
        it flies off to:
                a woman's world,
                        of crossed sticks, stopping
        thought. A new world
                is only a new mind.

> And the mind and the poem
>
> are all apiece.
>
> (PB, 75–76)

If a new world is only a new mind, then, of course, the old world
—the "life in which // two women agonize"—is equally a matter of
mind, and we have it in our power to transcend the old world by
simply reconstructing it imaginatively. The worm that is in our
brains, as Williams puts it later in the poem, is countered successfully only by the reorganization of thought that occurs in poetry.

Having established the problem and the means of solution, Williams proceeds with his meditation by recognizing that his feelings
are not unique. To some degree they must be shared by others, and
the mere recognition of this fact goes a long way toward mitigat-
ing the feeling of isolation:

> All women are fated similarly
>
> facing men
>
> and there is always
>
> another, such as I,
>
> who loves them,
>
> loves all women, but
>
> finds himself, touching them,
>
> like other men,
>
> often confused.
>
> (PB, 76)

Thus a parallel situation may be supposed to exist in the experience
of his sons, "who live also // in a world of love, / apart" (PB, 76).
By constructing an analogy between himself and his sons, Williams
moves closer to his sons' wives. In his own way, he—like his sons—
is drawn toward "a world of women"; and his sons, like him, are
somehow kept at a distance:

> Shall this odor of box in
>
> the heat
>
> not also touch them
>
> fronting a world of women

                              from which they are
          debarred
                    by the very scents which draw them on
                         against easy access?
                                   (PB, 76)

If the paradoxical combination of intimacy and distance that
characterizes Williams' relationship to his daughters-in-law is also
a feature of his sons' relationship to women, perhaps even with
respect to their own wives, then Williams has a basis for comparing
his love to theirs, a basis for assessing relative strengths and weak-
nesses. His own passion, he admits,

          is a love
               less than
                    a young man's love but,
          like this box odor
               more penetrant, infinitely
                    more penetrant,
          in that sense not to be resisted.
                                   (PB, 77)

Strictly speaking, his love for Daphne and Virginia is not a sexual
love, although it has strongly sexual overtones. It is "not the stress
itself" that concerns him but something "beyond / and above //
that" (PB, 77). There is, he says, a "counter stress,"

               born of the sexual shock,
                    which survives it
          consonant with the moon,
               to keep its own mind.
                                   (PB, 78)

It is this "that wants to rise / and shake itself // free," and it is this
that Williams struggles desperately to define. Just as "it" struggles
to transcend the limits of the sexual encounter, "the hard / give
and take / of a man's life with / a woman," so Williams, in his
effort "to come to speech at last," struggles to construct an address—a poem—that will transcend sex as an expression of his feeling.

As in "The Descent," he succeeds by converting his liabilities into assets. He cannot *make* love to Daphne and Virginia in the usual sense, but he can and does *assert* his love by expressing it in a poem. Moreover, in the course of composing his poem he comes to distinguish between these two different kinds of expression—the physical and the spiritual—so that the superiority of the latter can be recognized as an adequate compensation for the impossibility of the former. This distinction is the essence of the last section of the poem, which focuses on a pair of robins and a pet goose:

Staying here in the country
    on an old farm
        we eat our breakfasts
on a balcony under an elm.
    The shrubs below us
        are neglected. And
there, penned in,
    or he would eat the garden,
        lives a pet goose who
tilts his head
    sidewise
        and looks up at us,
a very quiet old fellow
    who writes no poems.
        Fine mornings we sit there
while birds
    come and go.
        A pair of robins
is building a nest ·
    for the second time
        this season. Men
against their reason
    speak of love, sometimes,
        when they are old. It is
all they can do ·
    or watch a heavy goose
        who waddles, slopping

> noisily in the mud of
> his pool.
>
> (*PB*, 78–79)

Unlike Williams, the penned-in goose writes no poems and is, therefore, condemned to a special kind of silence, which is only rendered more noticeable by his noisy slopping in the mud. The robins too are mute when it comes to poetry. Living as they do in total immediacy, caught up in processes they cannot understand or appreciate, they do not know, as Williams does, that they are building their second nest of the season. Even though they are properly engaged in an activity Williams can only talk about, nevertheless the power of his speech is such that it compensates for the diminution of sexual power. The robins must build their new nest from physical materials, but Williams can build a "new world" from the materials of his own mind. In that world, at least, Williams himself is the hero whose love is "infinitely / more penetrant" than a young man's love and "in that sense not to be resisted" (*PB*, 77).

In yet another example of the problem-solving approach, "To a Dog Injured in the Street," Williams brings himself, as he does in "To Daphne and Virginia," to a consideration of the power of his own mind by having to think his way around the implications of "the sorry facts." Although the poem's occasion is the objective reality of a suffering animal, the poem's true subject is the power of poetry to transform suffering—the poet's suffering, not the animal's. Faced with the painful spectacle of an injured dog, Williams retires defensively into the self, and from that point on it is precisely the virtue and flexibility of this maneuver that captures his attention:

> It is myself,
>   not the poor beast lying there
>   yelping with pain
> that brings me to myself with a start—
>   as at the explosion
>   of a bomb, a bomb that has laid

all the world waste.
        I can do nothing
                but sing about it
    and so I am assuaged
            from my pain.

                    (*PB*, 86)

If the odor of boxwood in "To Daphne and Virginia" is a healing
odor because it stimulates the writing of poetry, here the stimulus
of the wounded dog is also, paradoxically, healing because it en-
courages Williams to sing about it. That alone takes him beyond
the dog's condition, which, as Williams knows, is also his own
condition minus the power of reflection. Deliberately echoing
Keats, he writes: "A drowsy numbness drowns my sense / as if
of hemlock / I had drunk." This allusion is important, because it
makes the reader notice that Williams' poem is an almost perfect
inversion of the "Nightingale" ode. In Keats's poem, the speaker
is drawn irresistibly to a happy song far beyond his own powers,
a song poured out in "full-throated ease" by an animal that is more
than animal, a bird "not born for death." In Williams' poem, by
way of contrast, the speaker is repelled by the horrible yelping of
a dog apparently just struck by an automobile and at the point of
death. Whereas Keats yearns for an ecstatic union with the nightingale, Williams tries to interpose a barrier between himself and the
dog: "The cries of a dying dog / are to be blotted out // as best I
can." Keats's effort finally fails, and he is forced back into the painful limitation of ordinary self-consciousness. Williams, however,
succeeds in his effort precisely because he retreats self-consciously
into the depths of his own mind. One thought leads to another, and
soon he is far away from the immediate spectacle of the injured
animal:

                            I think
    of the poetry
            of René Char
                    and all he must have seen
    and suffered

```
                    that has brought him
                          to speak only of
        sedgy rivers,
             of daffodils and tulips
                  whose roots they water,
        even to the free-flowing river
             that laves the rootlets
                          of those sweet-scented flowers
        that people the
             milky
                  way   ·
                                      (PB, 86–87)
```

By contemplating a fellow poet's response to suffering, Williams demonstrates how thinking alone enables us to transcend a situation by extending its limits in any or all directions. In one sense it is surely outrageous to move so quickly in thought from the yelping dog to "those sweet-scented flowers // that people the / milky / way," but in another sense that is just the point. Metaphorical displacement or substitution, as Williams says in "To Daphne and Virginia," is a "resource" of the mind: "We // should be lost / without its wings to / fly off upon" (PB, 75). The question here is, what can one think about to blot out the cries of a dying dog? Maybe those cries have been mastered already on a previous occasion in a different form. Maybe the present spectacle can be linked with others in such a way that it loses its recalcitrance and becomes less debilitating (for Williams). This is exactly what happens when Williams reverts to two childhood memories involving the apparent suffering of animals:

```
        I remember Norma
                  our English setter of my childhood
                          her silky ears
        and expressive eyes.
                  She had a litter
                          of pups one night
        in our pantry and I kicked
```

```
                    one of them
                         thinking, in my alarm,
         that they
                    were biting her breasts
                         to destroy her.
     I remember also
               a dead rabbit
                    lying harmlessly
          on the outspread palm
                    of a hunter's hand.
                              As I stood by
         watching
                    he took a hunting knife
                         and with a laugh
          thrust it
                    up into the animal's private parts.
                         I almost fainted.
                              (PB, 87)
```

The gracious intervention of these memories gives Williams something to think about besides the "finality" which his senses would
otherwise be forced to "cling to in despair, not knowing which
way to turn" (*I*, 14). At the same time, these particular memories
illustrate what Williams says about memory in "The Descent."
Past experiences—even those as painful as the one in "To a Dog
Injured in the Street"—assume a new character when they are re-
viewed in memory. For one thing, it is now clear that Williams
was wrong about the calamity to which Norma had been sub-
jected, just as it is equally clear that Williams' response to the
hunter's gratuitous vulgarity was not shared by the dead rabbit. It
is at least possible, then, that even the present experience may be
revealed according to a new aspect when, at a later date, it is encountered again in memory. Conceivably it too may become part
of Williams' repertoire of experiences, to be drawn upon like a
bank account in some new calamity or whenever the need arises to
escape "our fearful bedazzlement with some concrete and fixed

present" (*SE,* 117–18). Indeed, the experience has already acquired a positive character to the extent that Williams already recognizes that his response to it—the writing of a poem about it—implies "the power of beauty / to right all wrongs." "With invention and courage," he exclaims, "we shall surpass / the pitiful dumb beasts" who are trapped permanently in the world of immediate experience. The dog's pain is inescapable; Williams' pain, on the other hand, is dissipated in the pursuit of its manifold ramifications.

In many, perhaps most, of his later poems, Williams is brought back to himself "with a start," just as he is in "To a Dog Injured in the Street." Everything he encounters is submitted to a process of thinking that eventually circles upon itself in order to reveal its own independent importance. Whereas the earlier poems appear to fan out in a thousand different directions to occupy a thousand different points of interest in a magnificent display of Keatsian empathy, the poems of the *The Desert Music* and *Journey to Love* repeatedly turn inward for the express purpose of recognizing one thing—the ego, the self, the "living flame"—as the ground of all significance and meaning. In these last poems, the heart (to use Hegel's terms again) "finds its manifestation in itself instead of in the external world and *its* form of reality, and this reconciliation with itself it can preserve or regain in every chance, in every accident that takes independent shape, in all misfortune and grief, and indeed even in crime."[3]

In "The Yellow Flower," we see with remarkable clarity the process whereby Williams' heart goes out to an unusual appearance of what in itself is no more than an ordinary flower. The crucial thing, however, is that in his thoughtfulness Williams extracts from the flower a lesson or moral concerning himself. Like the odor of boxwood or the injured dog, the flower contains, locked within its sensuous form, a wealth of implicit meaning which has to do primarily with the hopes and fears of the poet. By making this meaning explicit, Williams demonstrates how the flower can be interpreted as yet another occasion for self-assessment. Thus he converts the yellow flower into "The Yellow Flower," a poem that concerns itself finally with Williams' own power to escape the form of reality to which the flower must needs remain bound.

> What shall I say, because talk I must?
> > That I have found a cure
> > > for the sick?
> I have found no cure
> > for the sick   .
> > > but this crooked flower
> which only to look upon
> > all men
> > > are cured. This
> is that flower
> > for which all men
> > > sing secretly their hymns
> of praise. This
> > is that sacred
> > > flower!

>   (*PB*, 89)

This, of course, is the typical situation wherein an object of some sort impinges on the poet, attaining a momentary eminency for him that obliges him to point and to praise. "I must tell you / this young tree," "Young Sycamore" begins. Here Williams says, in effect, "I must tell you this crooked flower." But he does not construct his praise of it by giving his poem "over to the flower and its plant themselves," borrowing "no particle from right or left" (*I*, 19). He treats the flower as a complex of ideas—as a problem whose significance he must unravel. How is it that an "ungainly" flower, this particular "unnatural" flower, can mean something of such supreme importance that it merits the praise of all men? In what sense are we cured just by looking at it? Looking at the flower is easy; recognizing it for what it is or for what it means is quite another matter. What Williams wants is to decipher it.

"It is // a mustard flower / and not a mustard flower." It is "crooked" and "ungainly" with its "deformed" stem, and yet, at the same time, it is also a "sacred" panacea. The key to its mystery has to do with the fact that it manages to survive ("a single spray //

topping the deformed stem") under threatening conditions, far
from its natural habitat and out of its natural season. Its very existence "in this freezing weather // under glass" is anomalous:

> An ungainly flower and
> > an unnatural one,
> > > in this climate; what
> can be the reason
> > that it has picked me out
> > > to hold me, openmouthed,
> rooted before this window
> > in the cold,
> > > my will
> drained from me
> > so that I have only eyes
> > > for these yellow,
> twisted petals   .   ?

> > > > > (*PB*, 89–90)

The flower, then, is a paradox, a riddle, something for the mind
as well as the eyes. Like "the descent" into memory, which is
"made up of despairs" and yet "a reversal // of despair," which is
"without accomplishment" and yet "a kind of accomplishment,"
the yellow flower speaks of two opposite things simultaneously.
It speaks of "torture" and "escape" from torture in that despite its
crookedness and deformity it manages precariously to survive. In
this respect, the flower is clearly an image of Williams himself
facing a similar predicament, crippled by strokes yet living on in
spite of them. But the flower has more to it than this. If there is
"escape" through it, it is not simply because the flower has escaped physical extinction. Rather it is because Williams can use
the flower for meditation in order to transcend the condition of
"torture" he otherwise shares with it. Escape in this sense is not
available to the flower itself. Williams, in other words, does more
than just survive; he thinks of Michelangelo in much the same way
that he thinks of René Char in his poem "To a Dog Injured in the
Street":

                              It is
as if Michelangelo
        had conceived the subject
                of his *Slaves* from this
—or might have done so.
              And did he not make
                      the marble bloom? I
am sad
        as he was sad
                in his heroic mood.
But also
        I have eyes
                that are made to see and if
they see ruin for myself
        and all that I hold
                dear, they see
also
        through the eyes
                and through the lips
and tongue the power
        to free myself
                and speak of it, as
Michelangelo through his hands
        had the same, if greater,
                power.
                              (*PB*, 90–91)

The flower reminds Williams not only of the contorted bodies
that constitute the subject of Michelangelo's *Slaves* but also of the
sculptures themselves which reveal that the sculptor has gone up
over contortion and mastered it by means of his skill. Implicitly,
the mustard flower decoded, deciphered, means the power that
Williams brings to bear upon it to transform it into poetry. But
the flower contains this meaning only implicitly, only potentially,
apart from the poem that explicates it. Indeed, the point of the
poem is to liberate the meaning *of* the flower from its own implicitness *in* the flower, because, while the flower as an organism

is under siege and ultimately perishable, its meaning becomes imperishable as soon as it takes the form of an idea. "Which leaves," says Williams, "to account for,"

> the tortured bodies
> of
> the slaves themselves
> and
> the tortured body of my flower
> which is not a mustard flower at all
> but some unrecognized
> and unearthly flower
> for me to naturalize
> and acclimate
> and choose it for my own.
>
> (PB, 91)

The tortured bodies of the slaves themselves, the tortured body of the flower—what else can their fate possibly be but the fate of the injured dog, the fate also of Williams' own body? As bodies, they must all perish, but as ideas or meanings—as *exempla*—they exist forever in the mind that thinks them. In thought only are they "endless and indestructible" (PB, 74), like the dead Sibelius, who "has been born and continues to live in all our / minds, all of us, forever" (PB, 67). As Williams observes in "Tapiola," the mind alone is the place "where all / good things are secured, written down, for love's / sake and to defy the devil of emptiness" (PB, 67).

If, therefore, the task in Williams' earlier poetry is largely the task of finding an adequate embodiment of mind, of objectifying meanings and ideas by putting them into the form of facts and things, now the task is to liberate meaning from just such implicitness. If, as Emerson says, "the world is mind precipitated" (CE, III, 196), what Williams tries to do is to turn it back into mind again by making it assume the form of ideas. Furthermore, by means of his experiments in search of the new measure, he now makes poetry itself assume the form of meditative thought rather than the form of things—often to the consternation of those who

especially admire his earlier poetry precisely for its "thinginess."
This is not an abandonment of things, as might be feared. Instead,
by converting them into clusters of concepts, "hordes / heretofore
unrealized," which are infinitely explicable, Williams gives things
a place in the world of mind, canceling them only in the form of
pure sensuousness. Even words (being things) require such can-
cellation as Williams shows in "The King!" where it is clear that
the verbal definition of "Nell Gwyn" found in the dictionary—
"actress // and mistress of Charles the Second"—is misleading or
insufficient in its potential meaning by comparison to the explicit
meaning Williams develops in his interpretation of it. As it stands,
the dictionary's definition holds locked within it the manifold implications of what it means to have been Nell Gwyn. But what are
these implications? What does the definition, in fact, suggest besides the usual "pious rot" associated with the idea of a kept or
fallen woman? Before he can tell us, it is necessary for Williams to
do to the words of the definition what, thirty years before, he
claimed he had to do to the words of *Ulysses*. That is to say, he has
"to separate the words from the printed page, to take them up into
a world where the imagination is at play and where the words are
no more than titles under the illustrations" (*SE*, 28):

> She waked in the morning,
>   bathed in
>   the King's bountiful
>   water
>   which enveloped her
>   completely and,
>   magically,
>   with the grit, took away
>   all her sins.
>   It was the King's body
>   which was served;
>   the King's boards which
>   in the evening
>   she capably trod;
>   she fed

                    the King's poor
                        and when she died,
                            left them some slight moneys
                    under certain
                        conditions.
                    Happy the woman
                        whose husband makes her
                            the "King's whore."
                                                    (PB, 133)

Williams relieves our mental cramp by telling us what the words
"actress // and mistress of Charles the Second" mean to the man
of imagination, who, by virtue of his imagination, "knows all
stories / before they are told" (PB, 61). Although the meaning,
as Williams tells us, has been "preserved forever" in the seven
words that comprise the dictionary's definition, it is only an implicit meaning in that form. If the original words were truly adequate to express the depth of meaning contained within them without the benefit of Williams' commentary, he would not have found
it necessary to explicate them in his poem. Although they are potentially meaningful in themselves, they become actually meaningful only when they are converted or translated into the series of
thoughts that comprise Williams' interpretation of them.

   The crucial difference that Williams makes as an interpreter of
things, who alone has the power to give them "a full being" (I, 17),
is a difference that clearly elevates him far above the empirical reality he otherwise shares with his fellow men. In "The Host," for
example, the meal enjoyed in the railway restaurant by the white-
haired Anglican, the tall Negro evangelist, and the two Irish nuns,
is ironically a sacramental meal only for Williams, who is also in
the restaurant "chomping with my worn-out teeth" (PB, 93) in
unison with the others. All, including Williams, "proclaim" the
sacrament implicitly by their "common need" for the food as well
as by their enjoyment of it; but it is only Williams, the true priest,
who has the inclination to pronounce the words of consecration:
"There is nothing to eat, / seek it where you will, / but of the body
of the Lord." Without these words, the meal cannot be truly effi-

cacious in a spiritual sense, and the communicants are forced to partake of the host "witlessly." Since, indeed, Williams does not speak the words during the meal itself but only later in the act of writing his poem about it, the poem ends in a minor key:

> No one was there
> > save only for
> > > the food. Which I alone,
> being a poet,
> > could have given them.
> > > But I
> had only my eyes
> > with which to speak.
> > > > (PB, 94)

The poet's task, then, is to proclaim what is happening, not by participation but by declaring what things mean. Without understanding it, without grasping the idea of it, the well-fed Christians cannot be said to receive the full benefit of their meal. The moment in the restaurant is, therefore, a moment filled with potential meaning which becomes actual only in the poem that commemorates it.

We find virtually the same situation in "A Negro Woman." The woman who carries "a bunch of marigolds / wrapped / in an old newspaper" (PB, 123) past the store window brings beauty into the world, but she does so witlessly, like the religionists in "The Host," "not knowing what she does." Consequently, the meaning she bears with her is not available to her as it is to Williams, who, in pronouncing the words of consecration ("What is she / but an ambassador / from another world"), names her and lifts her out of implicitness into the idea. The importance of the naming process, the difference Williams makes because of his power to declare the woman's meaning, is demonstrated by the fact that the poem is divided into two equal parts, the first of which is mere description while the second represents the poet's act of interpretation. By releasing the meaning that is only implicit in the first part of the poem, the second part makes us aware that Williams' purpose is

not to describe what he has seen, to "repeat the thing without naming it" (*I*, 115); rather his purpose is to describe that process
whereby the world (as Emerson says) passes into the soul of man
"to suffer there a change and reappear a new and higher fact" (*CE*,
III, 21). To the extent that the poem makes us aware of this process by lapping over itself, so to speak, it enables us to see more
clearly than might otherwise be the case that Williams' consciousness of the woman, his receipt of her announcement, sublimely exceeds that which she is in herself.[4]

Indeed, Williams ascends to such a high plane of imagination in
these last poems that he is always able to draw on his own inner
resources to dispel the recalcitrance or opacity of the objects he
encounters. Since all works of the imagination are "interchangeable" (*PB*, 178), as he explains in "Asphodel," all may be assimi-
lated into the network of thoughts that guarantees the poet's independence of the limits attached to any one of them. "The senses
witnessing what is immediately before them in detail" (*I*, 14) do
not have to see a finality they must cling to in despair; they can see
whatever the poet wants them to see because his imagination is in
charge of them. Thus we have a poem like "Still Lifes":

> All poems can be represented by
> still lifes not to say
> water-colors, the violence of
> the Iliad lends itself to an arrangement
> of narcissi in a jar,
> The slaughter of Hector by Achilles
> can well be shown by them
> casually assembled yellow upon white
> radiantly making a circle
> sword strokes violently given
> in more or less haphazard disarray[5]

The fascinating thing about this poem is that it is so plainly false
on the level of common sense. There is certainly no intrinsic relation between the slaughter of Hector by Achilles and an arrangement of narcissi in a jar, whether painted or not. Nothing requires
us or constrains us to see the poem in the painting or, for that mat-

ter, the painting in the poem. But that is just the point. If there
were a compulsion or a constraint to see the one in the other so
that we could turn to our neighbor and say, justifiably, "You fool!
Don't you see that this painting of a jar of narcissi is really a representation of the violence of the *Iliad*?" we should be dealing with
precisely the sort of crude symbolism Williams rejects. As it is,
Williams can read the *Iliad* and think of a flower arrangement if
he wants to, just as he can also see a still life of a jar of flowers and
be reminded of the murderous encounters of Greeks and Trojans.
Either way, he establishes a crucial superiority to the object at
hand which frees him from the narrow possibilities it suggests at
first sight. Thus the idea of the *Iliad* that emerges from viewing the
flowers represents the poet's pursuit of the flowers' ramifications,
which are limited only by the scope of Williams' mind. By the
same token, the idea for a flower arrangement that comes to mind
as a result of reading the *Iliad* represents an extension of the poem's
possibility of meaning. Whichever way it goes, by virtue of their
association with each other, the object at hand and the object in
mind cross-illuminate each other. The flowers assume a new character when they are seen as a covert representation of violence,
while the violence itself is necessarily mitigated when it assumes
the aspect of a radiant circle of beauty. A "new world" is the result, subject only to the invention and courage of Williams himself, its sole proprietor. Ironically, "Still Lifes" is probably one
poem that could not be well represented by a still life or any other
painting and that is because its subject is an idea rather than the
embodiment of an idea in form or gesture. In order to arrive at the
generalization that all the imagination's works are interchangeable,
Williams has to have transcended particular instances in a manner
that no particular instance—no particular work of the imagination,
however metaphorical—could possibly reflect. Indeed, the actual
embodiment of the concept would require not one still life but an
infinite number of still lifes representing an infinite number of
poems. It follows, I think, that the value of the poem "Still Lifes"
is that it represents by its very form (i.e., the form of thought)
Williams' new freedom from the inherent limitations of all forms
of art, including the art of painting.

The poem, however, that most adequately reveals the transcendence of Williams' mind is "Asphodel, That Greeny Flower," in which Williams sifts through the "whole flood" of memories that constitute his inner life. The guiding principle in this poem is the love Williams feels for his wife and his need to reassert that love, which causes him to reflect on their lives together and on everything that has touched their lives. Nothing is excluded because everything Williams thinks of can be connected with his own need for reconciliation. The whole world, in fact, becomes a kind of gloss on his marital relationship and its fortunes. By drawing together in a single petition for forgiveness his hopes and fears, his recollections of books read, people known, paintings seen, and places visited, along with observations concerning their interconnections, Williams makes all subservient to the rule of his affection. Each of his thoughts becomes a "flower" given to Flossie in token of his feeling, proving that love "rules them all" (*PB*, 178) in that it "swallows up all else" (*PB*, 160). The priceless Goyas destroyed by fire in Buenos Aires, the Rosenbergs in the electric chair, Darwin's voyage in the *Beagle*, the man encountered in the subway, the vision of Herman Melville in the Hawaiian jungle, the spectacle of the atomic bomb, the spectacle of Flossie herself watering her plants—all of these are arranged side by side as parts of the bouquet. In the inner space-and-time that constitutes the medium of Williams' thoughts, everything keeps turning into everything else, and so all appears "as if seen / wavering through water" (*PB*, 162). If the poem becomes a sea, the sea becomes a garden. Love, which is both a garden and a sea, is also a flower, but then the storm and the bomb are flowers too, if the imagination takes them to be so. In Book III, the man in the subway who reminds Williams of his father disappears before Williams can speak to him. Thus he seems to be associated in Williams' mind with the failure of love, and we think back as we read to Williams' earlier remark in Book II that we "come to our deaths // in silence" (*PB*, 168):

> Speak to him,
>   I cried. He
>   will know the secret.

```
He was gone
        and I did nothing about it.
        With him
went all men
        and all women too
                were in his loins.
Fanciful or not
        it seemed to me
                a flower
whose savor had been lost.
                (PB, 173–74)
```

But immediately it becomes apparent that the savor of the experience is not lost on the higher plane of imagination when it is re-
hearsed in memory. As soon as Williams thinks about it, it becomes
"some exotic orchid" admired by Herman Melville in the jungle,
or "lilacs" belonging to the prehistoric cave dwellers of the Pyre-
nees. What was lost in the subway is regained in the poem, where
it releases the "hordes / heretofore unrealized":

```
And so, by chance,
        how should it be otherwise?
                from what came to me
in a subway train
        I build a picture
                of all men.
                (PB, 174)
```

In the end, of course, the chief obstacle to love is death—not the
fact of death but the fear of it, the idea of death. "The mere picture / of the exploding bomb," says Williams, "fascinates us / so
that we cannot wait / to prostrate ourselves // before it" (PB, 165).
But if death manifests itself as an idea or a concept, Williams has
the power to subject it to thought. He can "take it apart" (PB,
163). Between his awareness of death and death itself, between
"the flash // and the thunderstroke" (PB, 178), he can interpose
his own meditations. Instead of allowing death to possess his imagination, with invention and courage he can see to it that his imagi-

nation possesses death: "That gelds the bomb, / permitting / that the mind contain it" (*PB*, 179). As the poem concludes, Williams submits to one thing only, which he calls the "grace of the imagination," acknowledging as he does so a trinity composed of light, the imagination, and love, which "maintain // all of a piece / their dominance" (*PB*, 180). In thus reaffirming his own subservience to the power—"call it what you may!" (*PB*, 181)—by which he brings all things into spiritual subjection to himself, Williams ends where he began in "Love and Service" with a celebration of the mystery to which all the perishable signs ultimately refer, the one thing which is not interchangeable with any of its works:

I will, in fact, tell it against my very life itself, by which I make love greater than life, greater than knowledge. For it goes beyond life, where no knowledge goes and is the most daring of all the mysteries and the most wonderful, which is a sufficient pretext for the presence here of man. (*EK*, 185)

Notes

1 Idealism and the Vision of "The Wanderer"

1 " 'A Certainty of Music': Williams' Changes," in *William Carlos Williams: A Collection of Critical Essays*, ed. J. Hillis Miller (Englewood Cliffs, N.J.: Prentice-Hall, 1966), pp. 132–47.

2 *William Carlos Williams: An American Artist* (New York: Oxford Univ. Press, 1970), pp. 20–24, 168.

3 *The Shaken Realist: Essays in Modern Literature in Honor of Frederick J. Hoffman*, eds. Melvin J. Friedman and John B. Vickery (Baton Rouge: Louisiana State Univ. Press, 1970), pp. 45–71.

4 *The Inverted Bell: Modernism and the Counterpoetics of William Carlos Williams* (Baton Rouge: Louisiana State Univ. Press, 1974), pp. 60–65.

5 *Poets of Reality: Six Twentieth-Century Writers* (Cambridge: Harvard Univ. Press, 1965), pp. 285–359.

6 See especially Charles Altieri's *Enlarging the Temple: New Directions in American Poetry during the 1960s* (Cranbury, N.J.: Associated Univ. Presses, 1979). Altieri's distinction between the "symbolist" mode of the modernists, such as Yeats and Eliot, and the "immanentist" mode of the postmodernists, such as Olson, O'Hara, and Bly, roughly parallels the distinction Miller makes between the "romantic" poetics of transformation and the "modern" poetics of immediacy or presence. Similarly, Jerome Mazzaro, in *Postmodern American Poetry* (Urbana: Univ. of Illinois Press, 1980), associates modernism with an almost mystical attempt to overcome the consequences of our estrangement from original unity, whereas he interprets postmodernism as the expression of an "irrevocably worldly and social" attitude that takes things as they are without a sense of loss or alienation.

7 Some critics, including Altieri, trace modernism and postmodernism both back to their origins in the romanticism of the nineteenth century. Thus, according to Altieri, the "symbolist" mode appears to derive to some extent from Coleridge, while the "immanentist" mode derives from Wordsworth. In *The Poetics of Indeterminacy: Rimbaud to Cage* (Princeton: Princeton Univ. Press, 1981), Marjorie Perloff also traces the "two separate though often interwoven strands" of modern Anglo-American poetry back to the nineteenth century: "the Symbolist mode" of Eliot originating with Baudelaire and, ultimately, the "great Romantic poets," and "the 'anti-Symbolist' mode of indeterminacy" originating with Rimbaud. A third critic, Gerald Graff, detects "a continuous impulse from the beginnings of romanticism to the latest postmodernisms." (See especially his discussion of "The Myth of the Post-

modern Breakthrough" in *Literature Against Itself: Literary Ideas in Modern Society* [Chicago: Univ. of Chicago Press, 1979]). Although disagreements of this sort suggest the difficulty of locating precisely the date of postmodernism's emergence as an identifiable tradition, making the term itself of questionable value, nearly everyone agrees that the complex of ideas and attitudes Miller detects in Williams has become increasingly characteristic of modern culture as a whole.

8 Breslin, p. 21.

9 Somewhat confusingly, Riddel declares (in his essay in *The Shaken Realist*, p. 48) that "the sacrifice of ego is not a sacrifice of self, nor is it any comfortable resolution of the poet's essential alienation." Unlike Miller, then, who prefers to think of the poet's new relationship to his world in terms of an interpenetration of subject and object, Riddel thinks of it in terms of an ongoing effort to maintain contact through participation. In a similar fashion, Breslin claims that the sacrifice of the ego must be continually reenacted in order to remain valid (pp. 23–24). In fact, however, "The Wanderer" does not depict anything like a sacrifice of the ego.

10 Quotations from "Hyperion" and "The Fall of Hyperion" are taken from the Oxford Standard Authors Edition of Keats's *Poetical Works*, ed. H. W. Garrod (London: Oxford Univ. Press, 1956).

11 In Keats, the apotheosized poet (the poet as Apollo) may be observed in "Sleep and Poetry" in the figure of the charioteer who stands aside to contemplate the throng of thousands who "flit onward" in "a thousand different ways." Williams' role as a physician enabled him to adopt a similar stance with respect to his patients: "But the actual calling on people, at all times and under all conditions, the coming to grips with the intimate conditions of their lives, when they were being born, when they were dying, watching them die, watching them get well when they were ill, has always absorbed me" (*A*, 356).

12 This is one of the major contentions of the present study. Miller claims in *Poets of Reality* that idealism is one of the traditions that Williams turns away from. Likewise, Riddel observes that "resignation as a denial of the egotistical sublime, and ultimately of idealism itself, is manifest so obviously in Williams' poetry that it hardly needs commentary" (*The Shaken Realist*, pp. 48–49). Finally, Breslin associates Williams with a widespread revolt against "romantic subjectivity," perhaps the earliest expression of which was the imagism of Pound and Hulme. "Modern poetry," according to Breslin, "thus began as a radical repudiation of the romantic ego and the idealistic philosophy that supported it" (pp. 33–34). On the contrary, I should say that this assertion is extremely doubtful with respect to Pound and simply wrong with respect to Williams.

13 Gaudier's "Vortex Gaudier-Brzeska (Written from the Trenches)" appeared in *Blast* in July 1915 and is reprinted in Ezra Pound's *Gaudier-Brzeska: A Memoir* (New York: New Directions, 1974), pp. 27–28. After speaking contemptuously of the war as "this paltry mechanism,

which serves as a purge to over-numerous humanity," Gaudier turns his attention to the far more important mechanisms whereby he intends to derive and present his own emotions: the arrangement of surfaces. His ability to prevent the war from distracting him from aesthetic considerations, his ability to turn it to his own purposes, as for example when he carves his own design in the butt of an enemy rifle he has captured and dismantled, is analogous to Williams' ability to use the details of his own environment for artistic purposes without regard to their larger context or their conventional significance.

[14] "Preface," *The Quarterly Review of Literature*, 2, No. 4 (1946), 348. This prepublication review of a volume of poems by Byron Vazakas was also printed as the introduction to Vazakas' *Transfigured Night* (New York: Macmillan, 1946).

[15] *Biographia Literaria*, ed. George Watson (London: Dent, 1965), pp. 151–52.

[16] *Biographia*, p. 153.

[17] *Biographia*, p. 154.

[18] Although Williams objected mightily to the tyrannous effects of priestcraft in all its forms, his unwillingness to speak of God or of matters concerning the Divine has more to do with a mystical refusal to acknowledge separation from God than it does with a genuine atheism. As Emerson says, so Williams might also say: "That which shows God in me, fortifies me. That which shows God out of me, makes me a wart and a wen. There is no longer a necessary reason for my being" (*CW*, I, 82–83). To Williams' way of thinking, T. S. Eliot's zeal for being a wart and a wen was more sacrilegious than Williams' own reticence. In fact, talking "about" God was, as far as Williams was concerned, almost certainly a way of denying one's own participation in God. Thus, in a recently published letter to Richard Eberhart, dated 19 August, 1957, Williams writes: "I have always objected to the use of the godhead as a figure in a poem. If the total appeal is not to that, or That as you may prefer, it is completely tautological and redundant." By way of explaining this rather cryptic remark, Williams makes the following observation in another letter to Eberhart, dated 119 [sic] September 1957: "Since every important idea in our lives may be ascribed to God I do not in my poems want continually to ascribe them to the primal source. To do so is in my opinion tautological." See Richard Eberhart and William Carlos Williams, "Making Poetry a Continuum: Selected Correspondence," *The Georgia Review*, 37, No. 3 (1983), 533–64. The dimensions of Williams' religious mysticism will be made somewhat clearer in the next chapter.

[19] *Biographia*, p. 167.

[20] There are, of course, certain passages in Williams' prose that imply that the world *is* external or independent of the thinking mind, and these passages would appear to indicate that Williams is not an idealist. One of the most important of these often-quoted passages occurs in the prose of *Spring and All* when Williams speaks of a "world detached

from the necessity of recording it, sufficient to itself, removed from him [the writer of imagination], (as it most certainly is) with which he has bitter and delicious relations and from which he is independent" (*I*, 121). The context of this passage makes it clear that Williams' emphasis on the disjunction between writer and world is prompted by a desire to establish the independent authority or autonomy of the writer, not by a desire to claim that the world we experience is in any significant or ascertainable respect independent of our experience of it. Williams is, in fact, defending the idea that we can experience a work of art without seeing it as a reflection or representation of the world outside the work, just as we can experience the world around us without having that world filtered to us through the medium of representational art. In either case, however, *what* we experience cannot be detached or abstracted from the way *we* experience it. This is made abundantly clear in several other passages of the same text. For example, at one point in *Spring and All* Williams declares that "life becomes actual only when it is identified with ourselves" (*I*, 115). Later he speaks of "the only world of reality that men know: the world of the imagination, wholly our own" (*I*, 129). Indeed, to the extent that we are confronted with a world that, at first sight, seems apart from us, it is our duty to overcome this world, both in art and in life: "In the composition, the artist does exactly what every eye must do with life, fix the particular with the universality of his own personality—Taught by the largeness of his imagination to feel every form which he sees moving within himself, he must prove the truth of this by expression" (*I*, 105). In the last analysis, Williams has about as much use for a world outside of himself as the German idealists had for Kant's *ding an sich:* in certain contexts, it may be a useful fiction, but it is really a troublesome chimera.

21 Poetry, painting, philosophy, and science are all, as far as Williams is concerned, mental or intellectual processes. The products that result from these processes—poems, painted canvases, truths, and facts—are subordinate to that which produced them, which is why Williams maintains again and again in *The Embodiment of Knowledge* that the mind must learn "to conceive itself as standing beyond its processes" (*EK*, 42), that "the position of the mind is *outside* all categories" (*EK*, 52), and that, finally, "the individual himself" is the "unity . . . and the final term of all investigation" (*EK*, 73). It is this position of transcendence that makes man "the judge of all his own activities" (*EK*, 133), including the activity of constructing the different worlds of science, philosophy, and art.

22 G. W. F. Hegel, *Aesthetics: Lectures on Fine Art,* trans. T. M. Knox (Oxford: Oxford Univ. Press, 1975), I, 31.

23 *Aesthetics,* I, 101.   27 *Aesthetics,* I, 103.
24 *Aesthetics,* I, 101.   28 *Aesthetics,* I, 518.
25 *Aesthetics,* I, 102.   29 *Aesthetics,* I, 519.
26 *Aesthetics,* I, 104–5.
30 *Aesthetics,* I, 80. Hegel's broad use of the term "romantic" to desig-

nate virtually all of western European art since the triumph of Christianity does not make the term inapplicable or imprecise with respect to writers of the period generally known as romantic (Hegel's own period) or even with respect to modern writers such as Williams. In fact, the state of mind or spirit that Hegel terms romantic simply unfolds until it reaches its climax in the early nineteenth century. It is hardly to be doubted, moreover, that Hegel would have viewed modern art, had he lived to observe it, as an extension of this climax, as a mere exacerbation of the very same tendencies he noted in the productions of his contemporaries—tendencies which already suggested to him in the 1820s that, for us, art has reached the limit of its development and, indeed, already plunged into a state of dissolution.

[31] By calling Williams an idealist and associating him with the name of Hegel, I do not mean to imply that he was a confirmed Hegelian, nor do I wish to suggest that his views are strictly compatible with the views of any other systematic philosopher, such as Berkeley, Fichte, or Schelling. I do think, however, that Hegel's description of the waxing and waning of art in a series of stages is remarkably similar to Williams' account of the artist's progressive search for a completely adequate means of self-expression which, when found, ceases to be adequate. Thus Hegel and Williams both pay honor to the artist but, at the same time, they also insist that the work of art derives its value from the fact that it points to something beyond itself. How and why this is the case with Williams is the burden of the present study.

[32] "For a New Magazine," *Blues*, 1, No. 2 (1929), 31.

[33] "Notes from a Talk on Poetry," *Poetry*, 14, No. 4 (1919), 216.

2   Williams' Version of the Myth of the Fall and the Problem of Symbols

[1] They also make it plain that Williams was influenced more by Herbert Spencer than perhaps he remembered or cared to admit. In *Yes, Mrs. Williams* (New York: McDowell, Obolensky, 1959), he mentions that, as a boy, he read the philosophy of Spencer but was more impressed by Spencer's "habit of dictating to an amanuensis while in the act of rowing a boat" (p. 8) than by the content of Spencer's text. However, a comparison of "Love and Service" with Spencer's *First Principles* (New York: Appleton and Co., 1900) reveals that Williams' concept of the Unknown has much in common with Spencer's concept of the Unknowable, which is developed at length in Part One of *First Principles*. In fact, Williams' crucial emphasis on the importance of "forever changing the sign" so as not to confuse any particular sign with the mystery to which it refers is hardly distinguishable from Spencer's emphasis in the following passage from *First Principles*:

Very likely there will ever remain a need to give shape to that indefinite sense of an Ultimate Existence, which forms the basis of our intelligence. We shall always be under the necessity of contemplating it as *some* mode of being; that is—of representing it to ourselves in *some* form of thought, however vague. And we shall not err in doing this so long as we treat every notion we thus frame as merely a symbol. Perhaps the constant formation of such symbols and constant rejection of them as inadequate, may be hereafter, as it has hitherto been, a means of discipline. Perpetually to construct ideas requiring the utmost stretch of our faculties, and perpetually to find that such ideas must be abandoned as futile imaginations, may realize to us more fully than any other course, the greatness of that which we vainly strive to grasp. By continually seeking to know and being continually thrown back with a deepened conviction of the impossibility of knowing, we may keep alive the consciousness that it is alike our highest wisdom and our highest duty to regard that through which all things exist as The Unknowable. (pp. 96-97)

That Williams, having enunciated his own "first principles," turns his attention to the more practical problems of manipulating signs may be compared to the fact that Spencer, following his discussion of the Unknowable, proceeds in the rest of his philosophy to describe the dynamics of that which can be known.

[2] Williams has so many names for the mystery about which nothing can be said that he often reminds one of the paradoxical theology of Pseudo-Dionysius, who declares in his treatise *On the Divine Names*, trans. C. E. Rolt (New York: Macmillan, 1940), that "the Universal and Transcendent Cause must be both nameless and also possess the names of all things" (p. 62). In an effort to speak in some fashion about the Unknown, Williams calls it, among other things, the secret spring of all our lives, the strange phosphorus of the life, this rare presence, the radiant gist, the face of wonder, silence, the light, spirit, mind, force, imagination, a living flame, beauty, the intangibles, music, reality, truth, the thing we are. Moreover, the names we give to the ordinary things we encounter in our daily lives are necessarily, for Williams, secondary names for the Unknown. Since, as Pseudo-Dionysius says, "the Supra-Vital and Primal Life is the Cause of all Life," it follows that "we must draw from all life the attributes we apply to It when we consider how It teems with all living things, and how under manifold forms It is beheld and praised in all Life" (p. 146).

[3] "Advice to the Young Poet," *View*, 2, No. 3 (1942), 23.

[4] "A Note on the Art of Poetry," *Blues*, 1, No. 4 (1929), 78.

[5] Williams, "For a New Magazine," p. 31.

[6] "An Approach to the Poem," in *English Institute Essays, 1947* (New York: Columbia Univ. Press, 1948), p. 61.

[7] "To Martha Baird," 3 November 1951, *The Williams-Siegel Documentary*, eds. Martha Baird and Ellen Reiss (New York: Definition Press, 1970), p. 9.

[8] "A Note on the Turn of the View Toward Poetic Technique," *The Hanover Forum*, 5, No. 1 (1958-59), 62.

[9] See Williams' Introduction to Mimi Goldberg's *The Lover and Other Poems* (Philadelphia: Kraft Printing Co., 1961), pp. iv–vi.

[10] Reported in Emily Mitchell Wallace, *A Bibliography of William*

Carlos Williams (Middletown, Conn.: Wesleyan Univ. Press, 1968), p. xix.

11 Cited in Mike Weaver, *William Carlos Williams: The American Background* (Cambridge: Cambridge Univ. Press, 1971), p. 164.

3 Emerson the Precursor

1 That Williams was aware of Emerson can hardly be doubted, though it is impossible as well as unnecessary to establish the exact amount of Emerson's direct influence. Apart from the fact that much of Emerson can be imbibed indirectly through Whitman, one of Williams' lifelong favorites, it is likely that Emerson's *Essays* were among the volumes Williams read in his father's library along with *The Origin of Species* and *The Descent of Man*. It is worth noting, too, that Williams and his brother attended Sunday-school classes at the Unitarian church, which their parents helped to establish in Rutherford. As Paul Mariani points out in his new biography *William Carlos Williams: A New World Naked* (New York: McGraw-Hill, 1981), "Most of the members of the local Unitarian Society were in fact displaced New England Yankees . . . and the stress in classes was less on spiritualism and more on the formation of a well-developed, self-reliant intellectual perspective toward matters spiritual. It was, essentially, the same tradition that seventy years earlier had helped to shape Ralph Waldo Emerson himself" (p. 12). The important thing is not that Williams tried to follow Emerson slavishly (which of course he did not) but that Williams' whole way of thinking is demonstrably Emersonian.

2 Williams' phrasing in "Love and Service" is, in certain respects, analogous to Emerson's neo-Platonic phrasing in this famous passage which stresses the ultimate identity of that which contemplates and the object of contemplation. Thus Williams states that to the extent that we are "totally ignorant," we confront "the unknown." To the extent that we are "totally powerless in speech," the reality we would express is "silence." To the extent that we are filled with awe at the prospect of the mystery of existence, we may be said to "go about in the face of wonder."

3 See especially chapter 3 of Whitaker's suggestive study, *William Carlos Williams* (New York: Twayne Publishers, 1968), p. 63.

4 "Glorious Weather," *Contact*, No. 5 (June 1923), p. 1.

5 For a different view, see the chapter entitled "Transcendentalism and Imagism" in Tony Tanner's *The Reign of Wonder: Naivety and Reality in American Literature* (Cambridge: Cambridge Univ. Press, 1965). Using Williams to exemplify imagism, Tanner argues that while the transcendentalists and the imagists both "encouraged the incorporation of carefully contoured, objectively observed particulars into literature" (p. 87), they did so for different reasons. Whereas the transcendentalists were looking for God or "the All" in every discrete particular, the imagists, according to Tanner, were simply trying to estab-

lish points of connection between themselves and a world devoid of higher meaning: "In a world of melting beliefs, of disintegrating systems, a universe which seemed recalcitrant to one harmonious integrating explanation, the bewildered poet might take refuge in examining only the palpable fragment" (pp. 91–92). However apt this may be as a description of the motives of other imagists, it is clearly not appropriate to Williams. "I knew all—it became me" (*CEP*, 12) is not a cry of bewilderment, nor is the assertion "It is all // a celebration of the light" (*PB*, 181) an expression of doubt.

⁶ Williams too, it will be noted, is equally obliged to keep moving from object to object, since the eminency of every particular manifestation of the radiant "gist" is strictly temporary: "Its face is a particular face, it is likely to appear under the most unlikely disguises. You cannot recognize it from past appearances—in fact it is always a new face. It knows all that we are in the habit of describing. It will not use the same appearance for any new materialization" (*A*, 362).

⁷ *Aesthetics*, I, 594.

⁸ *Aesthetics*, I, 81.

⁹ Cited in Bram Dijkstra, *The Hieroglyphics of a New Speech: Cubism, Stieglitz, and the Early Poetry of William Carlos Williams* (Princeton: Princeton Univ. Press, 1969), p. 63.

¹⁰ "What Is the Use of Poetry?" cited in Dijkstra, pp. 75–76.

¹¹ "Measure—a loosely assembled essay on poetic structure," *Spectrum*, 3, No. 3 (1959), 155.

¹² *More Power: Report of the Newark Public Library, 1946–1952,* (Fall–Winter 1952), pp. 7–8.

¹³ It is perhaps worth noting that Williams anticipates in this respect the current subjectivist bias in literary interpretation. He would have sympathized, I think, with the overt idealisms of Stanley Fish and Harold Bloom and also with the covert idealism that occasionally manifests itself in the project called deconstruction.

¹⁴ Paul Mariani states in his biography (*William Carlos Williams*, pp. 714–16) that it was John Wingate, not Mike Wallace, who put the questions to Williams on the CBS television program "Nitebeat" on 4 September 1957. However, since Wallace himself may have devised the questions, and since a transcript of the interview appeared in Wallace's column in the *New York Post* (18 October 1957) under the witty title "Mike Wallace Asks William Carlos Williams Is Poetry a Dead Duck," I shall continue to refer to the meeting as Williams' interview with Mike Wallace.

¹⁵ The description here of the slow evolution of Tchelitchew's original experience—his contact with a tree in England—until it has become a finished work of art should be compared to Williams' admission in "Yours, O Youth" that contact with "an immediate objective world of actual experience" does not preclude modifications introduced by the artist's mind. In "begetting" a poem, says Williams, the mind works among stored memories until it "has drawn parallels, completed pro-

gressions, transferred units from one category to another, clipped here, modified there" (*SE*, 33–34). Furthermore, it may be said that this activity occurs willy-nilly whether or not the artist makes a deliberate effort, as he very well may, "not to pull out, transubstantiate, boil, unglue, hammer, melt, digest and psychoanalyze, not even to distill but to see and keep what the understanding touches intact" (*SE*, 233).

4 Poetry as Power

1 "A Note on Poetry," in *The Oxford Anthology of American Literature*, eds. William Rose Benét and Norman Holmes Pearson (New York: Oxford Univ. Press, 1938), p. 1313.
2 "A Retrospect," in *Literary Essays of Ezra Pound*, ed. T. S. Eliot (New York: New Directions, 1968), p. 5.
3 "A Retrospect," p. 11.
4 For a clear, illuminating discussion of the way in which Pound's aesthetic principles lead to poems that are precipitates or residues of mental action rather than mimings of mental action, see George Bornstein, *The Postromantic Consciousness of Ezra Pound*, Elizabeth Literary Studies Monograph Series, No. 8 (Victoria, B.C.: Univ. of Victoria Eng. Dept., 1977), especially chapter 4, "The Impact of Imagism."
5 *Gaudier-Brzeska*, pp. 86–89.
6 "A Retrospect," p. 4.
7 *Gaudier-Brzeska*, p. 92.
8 "Affirmations—As for Imagisme," in *Selected Prose, 1909–1965*, ed. William Cookson (New York: New Directions, 1975), pp. 374–77.
9 "Four Foreigners," *The Little Review*, 6, No. 5 (1919), 37. The "four foreigners" are Aldington, Dorothy Richardson, D. H. Lawrence, and James Joyce.
10 "To James Laughlin," 18 September 1942, "William Carlos Williams as Correspondent: Notes and Selections," ed. John C. Thirlwall, in *The Literary Review*, 1, No. 1, (1957), 16.
11 *Fifty Poets: An American Auto-Anthology*, ed. William Rose Benét (New York: Duffield and Green, 1933), p. 60.
12 This account of the poem's occasion is attributed to the director of the Rutherford Public Library by Geri M. Rhodes in her master's thesis, "The Paterson Metaphor in William Carlos Williams' *Paterson*," Tufts University, June 1965.
13 "To Benjamin Bailey," 13 March 1818, *Keats: Poems and Selected Letters*, ed. Carlos Baker (New York: Bantam Books, 1962), p. 424. Keats adds in this letter that "our Minds . . . are able to '*consec[r]ate whate'er they look upon.*' "
14 "To Lady Beaumont," 21 May 1807, *Literary Criticism of William Wordsworth*, ed. Paul M. Zall (Lincoln: Univ. of Nebraska Press, 1966), pp. 76–83. In explaining the psychological interest of this sonnet, Wordsworth gives a remarkably prophetic synopsis of the rationale that lies behind the procedures of imagism. Who is there, he asks,

that has not felt that the mind can have no rest among a multitude of objects, of which it either cannot make one whole, or from which it cannot single out one individual, whereupon may be concentrated the attention divided among or distracted by a multitude? After a certain time we must either select one image or object, which must put out of view the rest wholly, or must subordinate them to itself while it stands forth as a Head (p. 81).

With respect to the ship in his sonnet, Wordsworth observes that when it "comes forth" as an individual object, his mind is "awakened and fastened in a moment":

this Ship in the Sonnet may . . . be said to come upon a mission of the poetic Spirit, because in its own appearance and attributes it is barely sufficiently distinguished to rouse the creative faculty of the human mind; to exertions at all times welcome, but doubly so when they come upon us when in a state of remissness. The mind being once fixed and rouzed, all the rest comes from itself; it is merely a lordly Ship, nothing more:

This ship was nought to me, nor I to her,
Yet I pursued her with a lover's look.

My mind wantons with grateful joy in the exercise of its own powers, and, loving its own creation,

This ship to all the rest I did prefer,

making her a sovereign or a regent, and thus giving body and life to all the rest (pp. 81-82).

That Wordsworth finds it necessary to elucidate both the ship's and the sonnet's significance for the benefit of a perplexed admirer (Mrs. Fermor) is symptomatic of the difficulties posed by imagist poems a century later.

15 *Aesthetics*, I, 527.
16 *Gaudier-Brzeska*, p. 89.
17 "Four Foreigners," p. 38.
18 *Aesthetics*, I, 605-6.
19 See, for example, Williams' letter to Sylvia Beach, 24 June 1928, *Mercure de France*, 349 (August–September 1963), 114–16, in which Williams remarks that, "valuable as it is [i.e., *Finnegans Wake*], it is a development of but one theme which was touched on in Ulysses—one manipulative theme, that is. . . . I require a very explicit, limpid, flairingly truthful development of the meaning as contrasted with the all important words—from Joyce now."
20 "An Approach to the Poem," p. 63.
21 See, most recently, Marjorie Perloff's discussion of Williams' "French" decade in *The Poetics of Indeterminacy.*
22 *Aesthetics*, I, 602.   25 *Aesthetics*, I, 295–96.
23 *Aesthetics*, I, 600-1.   26 *Aesthetics*, I, 296.
24 *Aesthetics*, I, 601.   27 *Gaudier-Brzeska*, p. 92.
28 "Belly Music," *Others*, 5, No. 6 (1919), 26.
29 The importance of rhythm in verse as an indicator of the quality

of a poet's mind is stressed again and again by Williams. For example, in an essay called "Sequence and Change" he speaks of the "indispensable consonance" that ought to exist in a poem between "feeling" and "the words in position in the line," a consonance that comes from a writer's having made the subject of his poem "a personal possession." This personal possession of knowledge

is the thing that the reader looks for in what has been put on the page without which he finds nothing for him of deep interest. This is revealed by the variable quantity of the line (not wholly so, of course) of which I have been speaking. It is revealed above all by slight variations, slightly displaced emphases in the line structure (*The Literary Workshop*, New York, 1, No. 2 [1934], 52–53).

As Williams says in a foreword to Tram Combs' *Pilgrim's Terrace*, it is in "the metrical nature of the poem" that one finds "what the secret nature of the poet wants to communicate to us."

[30] "To Write American Poetry," *Fantasy*, 5, No. 1 (1935), 13.

[31] "The Fatal Blunder," *The Quarterly Review of Literature*, 2, No. 2 (1945), 125.

[32] "A New Line is a New Measure," *The New Quarterly of Poetry*, 2, No. 2 (1947–48), 9.

[33] "Vs.," *Touchstone*, 1, No. 3 (1948), 6.

[34] "A New Line is a New Measure," pp. 13–14.

[35] "Poetry and the Making of the Language: How Verse Forms Create Something New," *The New Republic*, 31 Oct. 1955, p. 17.

[36] *Aesthetics*, I, 80.

[37] *Aesthetics*, I, 525.

5   Thinking as Salvation

[1] *Phenomenology of Spirit*, trans. A. V. Miller (Oxford: Oxford Univ. Press), p. 19.

[2] Cited in Norman Malcolm, *Ludwig Wittgenstein: A Memoir* (Oxford: Oxford Univ. Press, 1958), p. 50.

[3] *Aesthetics*, I, 81.

[4] Indeed, the woman in this poem, like the ship that inspired Wordsworth's sonnet "With Ships the sea was sprinkled far and nigh," may be said to come "upon a mission of the poetic Spirit" because, like the ship, in her own appearance and attributes she is barely sufficiently distinguished to rouse the creative faculty of the human mind. On the other hand, in her role as ambassador, she has potentially the same spirituality Williams has. Thus she receives from him the honor he always gives to the people he observes in his poems who express themselves without knowing themselves for what they really are.

[5] *The Hudson Review*, 16, No. 4 (1963–64), 516.

Index

Abrams, M. H., 6
Adams, Henry, 67
Aldington, Richard, 87, 157n
Altieri, Charles, 149n
Arnold, Matthew, 23, 49

Baird, Martha, 50
Baudelaire, Charles, 149n
Beach, Sylvia, 158n
Benét, William Rose, 89
Berkeley, George, 153n
Blake, William, 40
Bloom, Harold, 156n
Bly, Robert, 149n
Bornstein, George, 157n
Bosch, Hieronymus, 75–76
Boyle, Kay, 47
Breslin, James, 3, 12, 150n
Burke, Kenneth, 49, 72

Calas, Nicolas, 75–76
Char, René, 133–34, 138
Coleridge, S. T., 22–25, 149n
Combs, Tram, 159n
Corman, Cid, 50
Crane, Hart, 6
Cummings, E. E., 71–72

Deconstruction, 156n
Dijkstra, Bram, 18, 156n

Eberhart, Richard, 151n
Einstein, Albert, 114–15
Eliot, T. S., 5, 47, 107, 151n
Emerson, Ralph Waldo, 6, 25, 38, 41,
    51, 53–77, 84–88, 90, 106, 109–10,
    117, 140, 144, 151n, 155n

Fichte, J. G., 153n
Fish, Stanley, 156n
Ford, Charles Henri, 71
Frost, Robert, 47

Gaudier-Brzeska, Henri, 18, 109,
    150–51n

God (god), 16, 24–25, 56, 100, 110,
    118, 123, 151n, 155n
Graff, Gerald, 149n

Hegel, G. W. F., 25–30, 51, 65–66, 90,
    98–99, 104, 106–9, 117–18, 124, 136,
    152–53n
Hulme, T. E., 150n

Icon, 38, 114
Iconoclasm, 37–38, 58, 114
Idolatry, 34–35, 42, 55, 57, 110–11
Imagism, 59, 63, 77, 81–101, 109, 112,
    117–18, 150n, 155–56n, 158n

Jarrell, Randall, 105
Jeffers, Robinson, 47
Joyce, James, 43, 47–48, 70, 101–3,
    107, 141, 157n, 158n

Kant, Immanuel, 152n
Keats, John, 3, 6–7, 13–18, 20, 90,
    133, 136, 150n, 157n

Laforgue, Jules, 72
Laughlin, James, 88
Lawrence, D. H., 157n

Macksey, Richard, 3
Mariani, Paul, 155n, 156n
Mazzaro, Jerome, 149n
Michelangelo, 138–39
Miller, J. Hillis, 4–5, 12, 149n, 150n
Modernism, 46–48, 62, 69–70, 87,
    149–50n
Monroe, Harriet, 28
Moore, Marianne, 70

New measure, 49–50, 77, 81–82, 111–
    19. See also Variable foot

Objective correlative, 19, 59, 88–90,
    123
Objectivism, 63, 77, 81–82, 99–112,
    117–18